# MATH PHONICS™

# DIVISION

## Quick Tips and Alternative Techniques for Math Mastery

### BY MARILYN B. HEIN

### ILLUSTRATED BY RON WHEELER

## Teaching & Learning Company

1204 Buchanan St., P.O. Box 10
Carthage, IL 62321-0010

# THIS BOOK BELONGS TO

_____

## ACKNOWLEDGEMENTS

I appreciate the support given to me by Kay Suchan. Special thanks to Lorraine Jeter for her suggestions about numbered cards and beads on a string.

## DEDICATION

I would like to dedicate this book to my husband, Joe; our children, Gretchen, Troy, Adam, Sarah, Robert, Nick and Jenny; and my parents, Vincent and Cleora Vestring.

Cover by Ron Wheeler

Copyright © 1997, Teaching & Learning Company

ISBN No. 1-57310-095-1

Printing No. 987654321

**Teaching & Learning Company**
**1204 Buchanan St., P.O. Box 10**
**Carthage, IL 62321-0010**

Math Phonics™ is a trademark registered to Marilyn B. Hein.

# TABLE OF CONTENTS

 **NOTE TO PARENTS**

Although this book has been specifically designed to be used by classroom teachers for teaching division facts, the materials are extremely helpful when used by parents and children at home.

If you have purchased this book to use at home with your child, I recommend that all of the fill-in-the-blank pages be inserted into vinyl page protectors and worked with a dry-erase overhead transparency marker. The page protectors can be washed and the page can be reused. Put all the page protectors and worksheets into a vinyl, two-pocket binder. The pen, flash cards and other materials can be kept in the binder pockets, thus creating a handy, portable math kit.

I think you will find that these methods work extremely well both at home and in the classroom. They have been tested and approved by parents and teachers!

# Dear Teacher or Parent,

*Attrition, refraction, stultification and revision!*

Lewis Carroll used some very similar words in the 1800s to describe the confusion and despair with which many students viewed mathematics. In the 1990s, it would seem that the more things change, the more they stay the same! We still hear complaints that too many students are progressing through school without a solid knowledge of the four basic math processes—addition, subtraction, multiplication and division. The most brilliant people who ever lived would struggle with fractions, decimals and every other math topic if they could not call to mind the basic math facts.

The Math Phonics™ series, including this division book, is a comprehensive approach to avoiding the common pitfalls that lie in store for students who need to master those math facts.

*Math Phonics™* has been used in elementary schools, homes and even in junior high and adult classes. One adult student observed the demonstration of Math Phonics™ as presented by the teacher, sat for a minute and then said, "Why didn't somebody show me this a long time ago?"

*Math Phonics™* is set up so that students will understand the basic concept before beginning to master the math facts. Since we fear what we do not understand, Math Phonics™ is a wonderful cure for math phobia!

Math is like a puzzle—a game for me. This *Math Phonics™* book is planned with a multisensory approach to learning and carefully designed games and activities for drill. These qualities can add a touch of fun to your math class.

Give it a try! This is a book you can count on!

Sincerely,

*Marilyn*

Marilyn B. Hein

# WHAT IS MATH PHONICS™?

Math Phonics™ is a specially designed program for teaching division facts initially or for remedial work.

## WHY IS IT CALLED MATH PHONICS™?

In reading, phonics is used to group similar words, and it teaches the students simple rules for pronouncing each word.

In *Math Phonics™*, math facts are grouped and learned by means of simple patterns, rules and mnemonic devices.

In reading, phonics develops mastery by repetitive use of words already learned.

*Math Phonics™* uses drill and review to reinforce students' understanding.

# HOW WAS MATH PHONICS™ DEVELOPED?

Why did "Johnny" have so much trouble learning to read during the years that phonics was dropped from the curriculum of many schools in this country? For the most part, he had to simply memorize every single word in order to learn to read, an overwhelming task for a young child. If he had an excellent memory or a knack for noticing patterns in words, he had an easier time of it. If he lacked those skills, learning to read was a nightmare, often ending in failure–failure to learn to read and failure in school.

Phonics seems to help many children learn to read more easily. Why? When a young child learns one phonics rule, that one rule unlocks the pronunciation of dozens or even hundreds of words. It also provides the key to parts of many larger words. The trend in U.S. schools today seems to be to include phonics in the curriculum because of the value of that particular system of learning.

As a substitute teacher, I have noticed that math teacher manuals sometimes have some valuable phonics-like memory tools for teachers to share with students to help them memorize math facts–the addition, subtraction, multiplication and division facts which are the building blocks of arithmetic. However, much of what I remembered from my own education was not contained in the available materials. I decided to create my own materials based upon what I had learned during the past 40 years as a student, teacher and parent.

The name *Math Phonics™* occurred to me because the rules, patterns and memory techniques that I have assembled are similar to language arts phonics in several ways. Most of these rules are short and easy to learn. Children are taught to look for patterns and use them as "crutches" for coming up with the answer quickly. Some groups have similarities so that learning one group makes it easier to learn another. Last of all, *Math Phonics™* relies on lots of drill and review, just as language arts phonics does.

Children *must* master addition, subtraction, multiplication and division facts and the sooner the better. When I taught seventh and eighth grade math over 20 years ago, I was amazed at the number of students who had not mastered the basic math facts. At that time, I had no idea how to help them. My college math classes did not give me any preparation for that situation. I had not yet delved into my personal memory bank to try to remember how I had mastered those facts.

When my six children had problems in that area, I was strongly motivated to give some serious thought to the topic. I knew my children had to master math facts, and I needed to come up with additional ways to help them. For kids to progress past the lower grades without a thorough knowledge of those facts would be like trying to learn to read without knowing the alphabet.

I have always marveled at the large number of people who tell me that they "hated math" when they were kids. I wonder how many of them struggled with the basic math facts when they needed to have them clearly in mind. I firmly believe that a widespread use of *Math Phonics*™ could be a tremendous help in solving the problem of "math phobia."

# WHAT ARE THE PRINCIPLES OF MATH PHONICS™?

There are three underlying principles of *Math Phonics*™.
They are: 1. Understanding
         2. Learning
         3. Mastery
Here is a brief explanation of the meaning of these principles.

**1. UNDERSTANDING:** All true mathematical concepts are abstract which means they can't be touched. They exist in the mind. For most of us, understanding such concepts is much easier if they can be related to something in the real world–something that can be touched.

Thus I encourage teachers and parents to find concrete examples of division facts. For example, a carton of eggs is an excellent example of $12 \div 2 = 6$. For $12 \div 4 = 3$, three rows of objects with four objects in each row can be arranged to demonstrate that fact.

Next we use the base 10 counting chart as a shortcut to the same answer. If a child has seen the division facts demonstrated by use of objects or the counting chart, she is much more likely to learn and master them.

**2. LEARNING:** Here is where the rules and patterns mentioned earlier play an important part. A child can be taught a simple rule and on the basis of that, call to mind a whole set of math facts. But the learning necessary for the addition, subtraction, multiplication and division facts must be firmly in place so that the information will be remembered next week, next month and several years from now. That brings us to the next principle.

**3. MASTERY:** We have all had the experience of memorizing some information for a test or quiz tomorrow and then promptly forgetting most of it. This type of memorization will not work for the math facts. In order for children to master these facts, *Math Phonics*™ provides visual illustrations, wall charts, flash cards, practice sheets, worksheets and games. Some children may only need one or two of these materials, but there are plenty from which to choose for those who need more.

# POCKET FOLDERS

You will want to purchase or create a pocket folder for each student to keep all the *Math Phonics*™ materials together.

Inexpensive pocket folders are available at many school or office supply stores, discount stores or other outlets.

An easy-to-make pocket folder can be made from a large paper grocery or shopping bag.

1. Cut away the bottom of the bag and discard.

2. Cut open along one long side and lay flat.

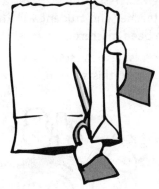

3. Pick one of the folds and measure out 10" (25 cm) from the fold on either side. Trim bag.

4. Now measure 12" (30 cm) down from the top and fold up the remaining portion of the bag.

5. Staple pockets at outside edges and fold in half.

6. Decorate front and back.

Suggest to parents that children should keep all of their *Math Phonics*™ materials (worksheets, travel folders, progress charts, etc.) in this folder. Parents may also wish to supply clear plastic page protectors and dry-erase markers. Worksheets can be inserted into the page protectors, completed with the dry-erase marker and reused. (See note on page 14.)

## 1. Teach the Concept of Division

In presenting Math Phonics™ to parents, I occasionally find an adult who says, "I started memorizing the division facts, but I had no idea what those numbers meant." We need to be sure students understand the concept of division before trying to memorize the basic facts. Materials are included in this Math Phonics™ program to clearly demonstrate and explain this concept.

## 2. Relate Division to Multiplication

If students have mastered the multiplication facts and understand the relationship of division to multiplication, learning division will be much easier.

Division is tricky because for each multiplication fact there are two division facts to be learned. For example, 6 x 8 = 48 gives two division facts: 48 ÷ 6 and 48 ÷ 8. To simplify the learning process, each time one group of division facts is taught–numbers divisible by six, let's say–we will also take the facts in which six is the answer. Those will be called the "matching facts."

## 3. Teach the Perfect Squares

Perfect squares are the division facts in which the divisor and the quotient are the same–16 ÷ 4 = 4, 25 ÷ 5 = 5 and so on. This is an extremely important group of facts and will be used often as students progress through their math classes. It's easiest to remember them if they are learned first, and they can be used as an aid in mastering later groups.

## 4. Divide by 9

The next group taught will be the 9s. This group is easy when students are shown the patterns in numbers divisible by nine. This knowledge will be helpful in reducing fractions and finding common denominators.

## 5. Divide by 2

We will next work with numbers divisible by two. Reviewing even and odd numbers is part of this lesson. Also students will be taught how to work with zero in division.

## 6. Divide by 4 and 8

These groups are closely related to the 2s and will be taught together in this step.

## 7. Divide by 5 and 10

The 5s and 10s can be learned in combination because they have common answers.

## 8. Divide by 3 and 6

These two groups are also closely related and will be learned together.

## 9. Divide by 7

This is a very difficult group for most students to master because it has no convenient pattern. It is taught last because every fact has been studied as a matching fact with one of the earlier groups. By using this process of elimination, students should have an easier time learning the 7s.

## 10. Review and Assessment

Constant review is very important in any area of mathematics, and several suggestions for review are given. Assessment pages are included so that the teacher and student will know when the facts have been mastered.

There is also a summary of games and rules included in this section.

# DIVISION FACTS

Facts in boxes are matching facts.

## Squares

1 ÷ 1 = 1
4 ÷ 2 = 2
9 ÷ 3 = 3
16 ÷ 4 = 4
25 ÷ 5 = 5
36 ÷ 6 = 6
49 ÷ 7 = 7
64 ÷ 8 = 8
81 ÷ 9 = 9
100 ÷ 10 = 10

## 9s

9 ÷ 9 = 1
18 ÷ 9 = 2
27 ÷ 9 = 3
36 ÷ 9 = 4
45 ÷ 9 = 5
54 ÷ 9 = 6
63 ÷ 9 = 7
72 ÷ 9 = 8
81 ÷ 9 = 9
90 ÷ 9 = 10

9 ÷ 1 = 9
18 ÷ 2 = 9
27 ÷ 3 = 9
36 ÷ 4 = 9
45 ÷ 5 = 9
54 ÷ 6 = 9
63 ÷ 7 = 9
72 ÷ 8 = 9
81 ÷ 9 = 9
90 ÷ 10 = 9

## 2s

2 ÷ 2 = 1
4 ÷ 2 = 2
6 ÷ 2 = 3
8 ÷ 2 = 4
10 ÷ 2 = 5
12 ÷ 2 = 6
14 ÷ 2 = 7
16 ÷ 2 = 8
18 ÷ 2 = 9
20 ÷ 2 = 10

2 ÷ 1 = 2
4 ÷ 2 = 2
6 ÷ 3 = 2
8 ÷ 4 = 2
10 ÷ 5 = 2
12 ÷ 6 = 2
14 ÷ 7 = 2
16 ÷ 8 = 2
18 ÷ 9 = 2
20 ÷ 10 = 2

## 4s

4 ÷ 4 = 1
8 ÷ 4 = 2
12 ÷ 4 = 3
16 ÷ 4 = 4
20 ÷ 4 = 5
24 ÷ 4 = 6
28 ÷ 4 = 7
32 ÷ 4 = 8
36 ÷ 4 = 9
40 ÷ 4 = 10

4 ÷ 1 = 4
8 ÷ 2 = 4
12 ÷ 3 = 4
16 ÷ 4 = 4
20 ÷ 5 = 4
24 ÷ 6 = 4
28 ÷ 7 = 4
32 ÷ 8 = 4
36 ÷ 9 = 4
40 ÷ 10 = 4

## 8s

8 ÷ 8 = 1
16 ÷ 8 = 2
24 ÷ 8 = 3
32 ÷ 8 = 4
40 ÷ 8 = 5
48 ÷ 8 = 6
56 ÷ 8 = 7
64 ÷ 8 = 8
72 ÷ 8 = 9
80 ÷ 8 = 10

8 ÷ 1 = 8
16 ÷ 2 = 8
24 ÷ 3 = 8
32 ÷ 4 = 8
40 ÷ 5 = 8
48 ÷ 6 = 8
56 ÷ 7 = 8
64 ÷ 8 = 8
72 ÷ 9 = 8
80 ÷ 10 = 8

## 5s

5 ÷ 5 = 1
10 ÷ 5 = 2
15 ÷ 5 = 3
20 ÷ 5 = 4
25 ÷ 5 = 5
30 ÷ 5 = 6
35 ÷ 5 = 7
40 ÷ 5 = 8
45 ÷ 5 = 9
50 ÷ 5 = 10

## 10s

5 ÷ 1 = 5
10 ÷ 2 = 5
15 ÷ 3 = 5
20 ÷ 4 = 5
25 ÷ 5 = 5
30 ÷ 6 = 5
35 ÷ 7 = 5
40 ÷ 8 = 5
45 ÷ 9 = 5
50 ÷ 10 = 5

10 ÷ 10 = 1
20 ÷ 10 = 2
30 ÷ 10 = 3
40 ÷ 10 = 4
50 ÷ 10 = 5
60 ÷ 10 = 6
70 ÷ 10 = 7
80 ÷ 10 = 8
90 ÷ 10 = 9
100 ÷ 10 = 10

10 ÷ 1 = 10
20 ÷ 2 = 10
30 ÷ 3 = 10
40 ÷ 4 = 10
50 ÷ 5 = 10
60 ÷ 6 = 10
70 ÷ 7 = 10
80 ÷ 8 = 10
90 ÷ 9 = 10
100 ÷ 10 = 10

## 3s

3 ÷ 3 = 1
6 ÷ 3 = 2
9 ÷ 3 = 3
12 ÷ 3 = 4
15 ÷ 3 = 5
18 ÷ 3 = 6
21 ÷ 3 = 7
24 ÷ 3 = 8
27 ÷ 3 = 9
30 ÷ 3 = 10

3 ÷ 1 = 3
6 ÷ 2 = 3
9 ÷ 3 = 3
12 ÷ 4 = 3
15 ÷ 5 = 3
18 ÷ 6 = 3
21 ÷ 7 = 3
24 ÷ 8 = 3
27 ÷ 9 = 3
30 ÷ 10 = 3

## 6s

6 ÷ 6 = 1
12 ÷ 6 = 2
18 ÷ 6 = 3
24 ÷ 6 = 4
30 ÷ 6 = 5
36 ÷ 6 = 6
42 ÷ 6 = 7
48 ÷ 6 = 8
54 ÷ 6 = 9
60 ÷ 6 = 10

6 ÷ 1 = 6
12 ÷ 2 = 6
18 ÷ 3 = 6
24 ÷ 4 = 6
30 ÷ 5 = 6
36 ÷ 6 = 6
42 ÷ 7 = 6
48 ÷ 8 = 6
54 ÷ 9 = 6
60 ÷ 10 = 6

## 7s

7 ÷ 7 = 1
14 ÷ 7 = 2
21 ÷ 7 = 3
28 ÷ 7 = 4
35 ÷ 7 = 5
42 ÷ 7 = 6
49 ÷ 7 = 7
56 ÷ 7 = 8
63 ÷ 7 = 9
70 ÷ 7 = 10

7 ÷ 1 = 7
14 ÷ 2 = 7
21 ÷ 3 = 7
28 ÷ 4 = 7
35 ÷ 5 = 7
42 ÷ 6 = 7
49 ÷ 7 = 7
56 ÷ 8 = 7
63 ÷ 9 = 7
70 ÷ 10 = 7

# LESSON PLAN 1

**OBJECTIVE:** Understanding division. Students will gain an understanding of the basic concept of division by use of concrete examples.

**MATERIALS:** five bowls and 15 counters (optional), enlarged and laminated Base 10 Counting Chart for wall, Worksheets A and B (pages 12 and 13), parents' note (page 14), Optional Notes (page 15), Base 10 Counting Chart (page 95)

**INTRODUCTION:** This step will immediately put division into a concrete situation so students can grasp the meaning. There are several methods which can be used to explain the process of division. *It is not necessary to use all five methods!*

Mrs. Jones has 15 cookies. She wants to divide them evenly among her five children. How many cookies will each child get?

**METHOD 1:** Have 15 students stand at the front of the room. They are the cookies. Draw five large circles on the board. These are the plates for the cookies. Distribute the students evenly across the circles one at a time until there are three in front of each circle. This shows that:

$$15 \div 5 = 3$$

**NOTE:** At this time, point out to students what the division sign looks like. The number before the sign tells how many items are to be divided. The second tells what number you are dividing by in this problem.

**METHOD 3:** For a simpler method, draw five circles on the board and distribute 15 Xs evenly among the circles.

**METHOD 4:** Use the Base 10 Counting Chart. Circle groups of five numbers ending with 15. There are three groups of five, so each child gets three cookies.

**METHOD 5:** Put a rectangular array of 15 Xs on the board.

X X X X X
X X X X X
X X X X X

Circle groups of 5 Xs. There are three groups. All these methods demonstrate that:

$$15 \div 5 = 3$$

Use additional examples if necessary.

**NOTE:** If students will be using a Base 10 Counting Chart, give each one a vinyl page protector and dry-erase marker so that the chart can be reused.

**METHOD 2:** Use five bowls at a table at the front of the room. Use 15 round counters such as pennies, poker chips, cardboard circles or milk jug lids for the cookies. (You could use real cookies!) Distribute the counters evenly among the bowls. Have a student come and see that there are three in each bowl.

# LESSON PLAN 1

**ASSIGNMENT:** Worksheets A and B.

**TAKE-HOME:** Have the students interview parents or friends and see how many ways they use division in their homes and jobs. Students should write at least three examples and bring them to school the following day.

Ask for a volunteer to call the local TV station and ask the sportscaster how division is used to find statistics on individual players in baseball, football and other sports. (One example would be a baseball player's batting average.) Another volunteer might speak to the weather forecaster about average temperatures, rainfall, snowfall, windchill, humidity, etc.

Other students might be more interested in how shoe and clothing manufacturers determine what standard sizes should be. Those change from one generation to the next based upon average measurements. They are determined by use of division.

**ENRICHMENT:** Recall the demonstration with the bowls and counters. Ancient people who were unable to write would probably have used this type of division all the time. We could use it in our lives today if we wished. However, imagine a division problem like this:

$$5,000 \div 25 = ?$$

You would need 5,000 markers and 25 bowls! That would be awkward and time-consuming. It is much easier to do written division problems. This is an example of why we learn the division facts.

**CHALLENGE:** Tell students to make educated guesses on the challenge problems at the bottom of Worksheets A and B. When checking those problems, demonstrate the correct answer by use of addition. $60 \div 3$ seems like it should be 20 and it is because

$$20 + 20 + 20 = 60$$

Dividing 60 into three groups, you have 20 in each group.

**PARENTS' NOTE:** Send home the note on page 14. Use Optional Notes on page 15 if desired.

# DIVISION PRACTICE

Count the Xs in each group. Put that number in the box. The number after the division sign tells how many rows there are. Circle rows of Xs. Count the circled groups. Put that number in the triangle.

1.  X X X X
    X X X X      12 ÷ **3** = 4
    X X X X

2.  X X X X X
    X X X X X
    X X X X X      20 ÷ **4** = 5
    X X X X X

3.  X X X X X X      36 ÷ **6** = 6
    X X X X X X
    X X X X X X
    X X X X X X
    X X X X X X
    X X X X X X

4.  X X X X X X
    X X X X X X      18 ÷ **3** = 6
    X X X X X X

5.  X X X X X      25 ÷ **5** = 5
    X X X X X
    X X X X X
    X X X X X
    X X X X X

6.  X X X X X X X X      32 ÷ **4** = 8
    X X X X X X X X
    X X X X X X X X
    X X X X X X X X

For each division problem, make a rectangular array of Xs on the back of this page or use a Base 10 Counting Chart and circle the groups to find the answer.

7.  12 ÷ 4 = __3__    8.  15 ÷ 3 = __5__    9.  25 ÷ 5 = __5__    10. 6 ÷ 3 = __3__

11. 8 ÷ 4 = __2__    12. 10 ÷ 2 = __5__    13. 16 ÷ 4 = __4__    14. 18 ÷ 2 = __9__

15. Mary's class has 36 desks. They want to arrange them in 6 rows. How many desks will be in each row?

16. Jim knows it is 35 days until his birthday. How many weeks would that be?

**CHALLENGE:** Try these larger numbers.

a. 60 ÷ 3 = ____    b. 80 ÷ 4 = ____    c. 60 ÷ 2 = ____    d. 80 ÷ 2 = ____    e. 90 ÷ 3 = ____

# MORE DIVISION PRACTICE

Count the Xs in each group. Put that number in the box. The number after the division sign tells how many rows there are. Circle rows of Xs. Count the circled groups. Put that number in the triangle.

1.
```
X X X X X
X X X X X
X X X X X
X X X X X
X X X X X
```
$\boxed{25} \div \mathbf{5} = \triangle 5$

2.
```
X X X X X
X X X X X
X X X X X
X X X X X
```
$\boxed{20} \div \mathbf{4} = \triangle 5$

3.
```
X X X X
X X X X
X X X X
X X X X
X X X X
X X X X
```
$\boxed{24} \div \mathbf{6} = \triangle 4$

4.
```
X X X X
X X X X
X X X X
```
$\boxed{12} \div \mathbf{3} = \triangle 4$

Use rectangular array or Base 10 Counting Chart to find the answers.

5.  $6 \div 2 = \underline{3}$      6.  $6 \div 3 = \underline{\phantom{00}}$      7.  $9 \div 3 = \underline{\phantom{00}}$      8.  $4 \div 2 = \underline{\phantom{00}}$

9.  $16 \div 4 = \underline{4}$      10. $25 \div 5 = \underline{\phantom{00}}$      11. $18 \div 2 = \underline{\phantom{00}}$      12. $27 \div 3 = \underline{\phantom{00}}$

13. $27 \div 9 = \underline{\phantom{00}}$      14. $21 \div 3 = \underline{\phantom{00}}$      15. $21 \div 7 = \underline{\phantom{00}}$      16. $12 \div 3 = \underline{\phantom{00}}$

17. $12 \div 4 = \underline{3}$      18. $35 \div 5 = \underline{\phantom{00}}$      19. $35 \div 7 = \underline{\phantom{00}}$      20. $36 \div 6 = \underline{\phantom{00}}$

21. In gym class, there are 16 shoes in a pile in the locker room. How many pairs of shoes are in the pile?

22. Twelve students have entered the science fair. If there are 3 students on each team, how many teams will there be?

**CHALLENGE:** Try these problems.

a.  $180 \div 2 = \underline{\phantom{000}}$      b.  $270 \div 3 = \underline{\phantom{000}}$      c.  $350 \div 5 = \underline{\phantom{000}}$

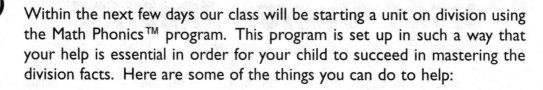

# DEAR PARENTS,

Within the next few days our class will be starting a unit on division using the Math Phonics™ program. This program is set up in such a way that your help is essential in order for your child to succeed in mastering the division facts. Here are some of the things you can do to help:

1. Help your child find a good place to post the Travel Folders so that they will give a visual image to help master the facts on the folder. Some ideas would be on a mirror, the side of the fridge or on the wall near the light switch in the bedroom.

2. Verbally quiz your child from time to time, perhaps while you are fixing supper or driving in the car.

3. When your son or daughter has learned one group of facts, sign the appropriate space on the progress chart which will be sent home.

4. Once or twice a week, play one of the games your child has learned at school to reinforce the facts.

5. Once your child has learned several of the groups, review the first few groups once every week or two.

Please keep all the Math Phonics™ materials (worksheets, travel folders, progress charts, etc.) in the folder which your child has brought home. You may wish to purchase a clear plastic page protector and a dry-erase marker. Worksheets can be inserted in to the page protector, completed with the dry-erase marker and reused.

The Math Phonics™ program relies on teaching children patterns in the groups of division facts. Visual images on wall posters, verbal and written review and lots of practice in the form of flash cards and games are ways to help children learn and recall these patterns.

Sincerely,

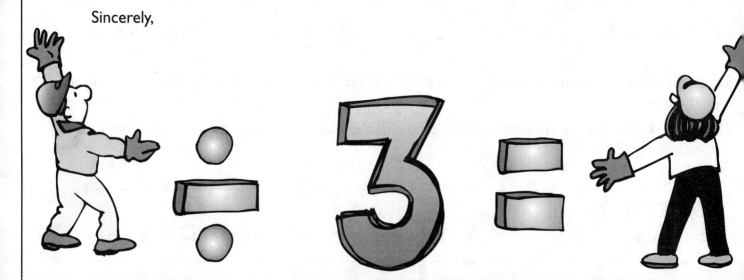

I am interested in attending a Math Phonics™ training meeting.

**Name:** _____

**Address:** _____

**Phone:** _____

I am available at these times: _____

---

**Dear Parents,**

The Math Phonics™ training meeting will be held:

**Date:** _____

**Time:** _____

**Place:** _____

Please bring the pocket folder and all the Travel Folders, Practice Facts sheets and Worksheets which your child has brought home. The meeting will be over in 30 minutes, but you may stay a little longer if you have questions.

Sincerely,

# LESSON PLAN 2

**OBJECTIVE:** Division as related to multiplication. Students will understand the relationship between division and multiplication. They will begin to use the multiplication facts they already know to find division answers.

**MATERIALS:** Multiplication Assessment sheets (pages 17 and 18), Worksheets C and D (pages 20 and 21), Base 10 Counting Chart (page 95)

**INTRODUCTION:** Students should share the division examples they brought from home. Spend a few minutes discussing the importance of this skill in the real world.

Check to be sure that students recall the multiplication facts. Use the Multiplication Assessment sheets.

For any facts that are missed, use materials from *Math Phonics™–Multiplication* or other materials for review. For students who need extra review, find parents or older students who can help.

*Students need to know the multiplication facts before starting division.*

**HOMEWORK:** Worksheets C and D.

**EXTRA CREDIT:** If students wish, they could learn to spell *inverse functions* and write it on the back of Worksheet D for extra credit.

**NOTE:** When checking the challenge on Worksheet D (page 21), demonstrate the answers with addition. 80 ÷ 2 = 40 because

$$40 + 40 = 80$$

**POSTER:** Page 19 is a mini poster which can be enlarged, laminated and posted in the classroom. The purpose is to help students learn to spell *inverse functions*, and the three terms used for a division problem—*dividend*, *divisor* and *quotient* which will be explained in Lesson Plan 3.

**DIVISION DEMONSTRATION:** This demonstration will show students that multiplication and division are opposites of each other. (*Inverse function* is the correct mathematical term, but *opposite* is an appropriate term for young students.)

**DEMONSTRATION:** Tran has mowed 4 lawns and received $5 for each lawn. How much money has he in all? (Use a rectangular array if necessary, but students should know this.)

4 x 5 = 20

Tran wants to buy 4 gifts. He wants to spend the same amount on each gift. How much can he spend on each one?

20 ÷ 4 = ?

Use the Base 10 Counting Chart. Circle groups of 4 and stop at 20. How many groups? Five. Thus we know:

20 ÷ 4 = 5

If he bought 5 gifts, we would circle groups of 5 and get 20 ÷ 5 = 4.

Compare the three problems:

4 x 5 = 20     20 ÷ 5 = 4     20 ÷ 4 = 5

Use other examples if necessary.

**RULE:** The three numbers in a multiplication problem can be used to form division facts.

**NOTE:** The word *pogs* is used in number 14 of Worksheet C. If pogs are not popular in your area, tell the class that pogs are circular cardboard lids that are printed with designs. They are saved and traded by some students in much the same way that people save and trade baseball cards.

# MULTIPLICATION ASSESSMENT

1. 12 x 2 = ___          2. 11 x 6 = ___          3. 0 x 1 = ___

4. 3 x 1 = ___          5. 12 x 3 = ___          6. 2 x 2 = ___

7. 11 x 3 = ___          8. 0 x 0 = ___          9. 7 x 5 = ___

10. 6 x 9 = ___          11. 5 x 6 = ___          12. 10 x 4 = ___

13. 8 x 7 = ___          14. 7 x 7 = ___          15. 1 x 2 = ___

16. 2 x 5 = ___          17. 3 x 4 = ___          18. 4 x 0 = ___

19. 0 x 2 = ___          20. 1 x 6 = ___          21. 9 x 4 = ___

22. 10 x 6 = ___          23. 5 x 3 = ___          24. 10 x 7 = ___

25. 8 x 8 = ___          26. 7 x 4 = ___          27. 5 x 8 = ___

28. 4 x 6 = ___          29. 12 x 6 = ___          30. 1 x 1 = ___

31. 9 x 9 = ___          32. 10 x 11 = ___          33. 2 x 6 = ___

34. 4 x 2 = ___          35. 3 x 3 = ___          36. 11 x 8 = ___

37. 7 x 9 = ___          38. 3 x 0 = ___          39. 11 x 11 = ___

40. 9 x 8 = ___          41. 9 x 5 = ___          42. 2 x 3 = ___

43. 10 x 10 = ___          44. 4 x 8 = ___          45. 10 x 5 = ___

**17**

# MULTIPLICATION ASSESSMENT

46. **11** x **6** = ___   47. **8** x **2** = ___   48. **3** x **8** = ___

49. **0** x **5** = ___   50. **11** x **2** = ___   51. **12** x **0** = ___

52. **6** x **3** = ___   53. **0** x **8** = ___   54. **11** x **2** = ___

55. **11** x **9** = ___   56. **10** x **3** = ___   57. **4** x **4** = ___

58. **1** x **4** = ___   59. **9** x **1** = ___   60. **11** x **1** = ___

61. **11** x **5** = ___   62. **2** x **9** = ___   63. **5** x **1** = ___

64. **12** x **8** = ___   65. **6** x **8** = ___   66. **11** x **0** = ___

67. **10** x **1** = ___   68. **10** x **8** = ___   69. **9** x **3** = ___

70. **10** x **9** = ___   71. **10** x **12** = ___   72. **5** x **5** = ___

73. **2** x **7** = ___   74. **1** x **8** = ___   75. **12** x **9** = ___

76. **12** x **12** = ___   77. **9** x **0** = ___   78. **6** x **6** = ___

79. **3** x **7** = ___   80. **10** x **2** = ___   81. **10** x **10** = ___

82. **12** x **7** = ___   83. **11** x **4** = ___   84. **12** x **1** = ___

85. **1** x **7** = ___   86. **7** x **6** = ___   87. **12** x **4** = ___

88. **12** x **5** = ___   89. **5** x **4** = ___   90. **7** x **0** = ___

# MULTIPLICATION AND DIVISION ARE INVERSE FUNCTIONS

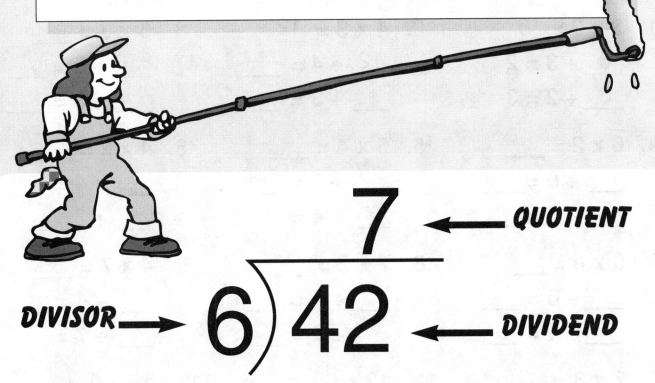

$$7 \quad \longleftarrow \text{QUOTIENT}$$

$$\text{DIVISOR} \longrightarrow 6\overline{)42} \quad \longleftarrow \text{DIVIDEND}$$

$$\text{DIVIDEND} \longrightarrow 42 \div 6 = 7 \longleftarrow \text{QUOTIENT}$$

$$\uparrow$$
$$\text{DIVISOR}$$

# MULTIPLICATION AND DIVISION

1. **3 x 2 =** _6_

   _6_ **÷ 3 = 2**

   _6_ **÷ 2 = 3**

2. **4 x 3 =** _12_

   _12_ **÷ 4 =** ___

   ___ **÷ 3 =** ___

3. **5 x 3 =** ___

   ___ **÷ 5 =** ___

   ___ **÷ 3 =** ___

4. **6 x 2 =** ___

   ___ **÷ 6 =** ___

   ___ **÷ 2 =** ___

5. **5 x 4 =** ___

   ___ **÷ 5 =** ___

   ___ **÷ 4 =** ___

6. **4 x 2 =** ___

   ___ **÷ 4 =** ___

   ___ **÷ 2 =** ___

7. **6 x 4 =** ___

   ___ **÷ 6 =** ___

   ___ **÷ 4 =** ___

8. **7 x 2 =** ___

   ___ **÷ 7 =** ___

   ___ **÷ 2 =** ___

9. **4 x 7 =** ___

   ___ **÷ 4 =** ___

   ___ **÷ 7 =** ___

10. **7 x 3 =** ___

    ___ **÷ 7 =** ___

    ___ **÷ 3 =** ___

11. **12 ÷ 6 =** ___

12. **15 ÷ 3 =** ___

13. **20 ÷ 4 =** ___

14. John has collected 27 pogs. He keeps an equal number in each of 3 containers. How many pogs are in each container?

15. Karen has 16 hair ribbons. She wears two different ribbons each day. How many days will it take her to wear them all? (She never wears the same ribbon twice!)

**CHALLENGE:** Anna is selling cookies. Each day she sells twice as many as the day before. If she sells two on day one, how many does she sell on day five? After seven days, how many cookies has she sold in all?

## MULTIPLICATION AND DIVISION

1.  **5 x 2 =** _10_
    _10_ **÷ 5 = 2**
    _10_ **÷ 2 = 5**

2.  **6 x 8 =** ___
    ___ **÷ 6 = 8**
    ___ **÷ 8 =** ___

3.  **2 x 8 =** ___
    ___ **÷ 2 =** ___
    ___ **÷ 8 =** ___

4.  **8 x 7 =** ___
    ___ **÷ 8 =** ___
    ___ **÷ 7 =** ___

5.  **8 x 1 =** ___
    ___ **÷ 8 =** ___
    ___ **÷ 1 =** ___

6.  **7 x 9 =** ___
    ___ **÷ 7 =** ___
    ___ **÷ 9 =** ___

7.  **9 x 6 =** ___
    ___ **÷ 9 =** ___
    ___ **÷ 6 =** ___

8.  **9 x 2 =** ___
    ___ **÷ 9 =** ___
    ___ **÷ 2 =** ___

9.  **9 x 8 =** ___
    ___ **÷ 9 =** ___
    ___ **÷ 8 =** ___

10. **10 x 9 =** ___
    ___ **÷ 10 =** ___
    ___ **÷ 9 =** ___

11. **8 ÷ 4 =** ___

12. **14 ÷ 7 =** ___

13. **80 ÷ 8 =** ___

14. **12 ÷ 6 =** ___

15. **15 ÷ 3 =** ___

16. **10 ÷ 2 =** ___

17. Mrs. Ruiz has 18 shoes. How many pairs of shoes does she have?

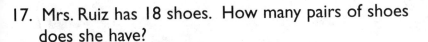

**CHALLENGE:**
a. 80 ÷ 2 = _____    b. 800 ÷ 2 = _____    c. 600 ÷ 2 = _____

**EXTRA CHALLENGE:** On the back, write and correctly spell the two words that complete this sentence. Multiplication and division are _____ _____.

**OBJECTIVE:** Students will learn the perfect squares as division facts and begin to use the division bracket.

**MATERIALS:** page protectors and markers, Perfect Squares sheet (page 24), Flash Cards (pages 25-34), Practice Facts for Squares (page 35), Travel Folder for Squares (page 36), Worksheets E and F (pages 37 and 38), Base 10 Counting Chart (page 95)

**INTRODUCTION:** Perfect squares are multiplication facts in which the two numbers being multiplied (or factors) are the same—2 x 2 = 4, 3 x 3 = 9 and so on. There are several reasons for teaching squares first. One is their importance in solving quadratic equations in algebra and right triangles in trigonometry. They are spaced far apart on the number line and are easier to master if learned first. They are helpful in learning some of the harder groups. For these reasons, perfect squares will also be studied first in division.

**Example:** If necessary, use the Base 10 Counting Chart or a rectangular array to demonstrate that:

$$8 \times 8 = 64 \text{ and } 64 \div 8 = 8$$

Ask students for other perfect squares facts (page 9) and the corresponding division facts. (Use the Perfect Squares sheet if you wish.)

**BRACKET:** Introduce the division bracket. A division problem can be written as:

$$64 \div 8 = 8 \text{ or } \quad 8\overline{)64}$$

Be sure students know that for now, the largest number goes inside the bracket. (That is not always true, but we won't deal with decimals and fractions at this time.)

**TERMS:** The three terms in a division problem can be very tricky to remember. You may prefer not to teach these terms, but it is easier to talk about a division problem if everyone uses the correct terms. Here are some hints to help students remember which term is which.

**DIVIDEND:** This is the largest number and is inside the bracket. The **dividend** is the largest number to the left of the division sign or inside the division bracket.

**DIVISOR:** The ending sound of this word is helpful. The divis**or** is the one that does the dividing, just as a teach**er** is the one who does the teaching, and the employ**er** is the one who does the employing. The **divisor** is the number to the right of the division sign, or in front of the bracket.

**QUOTIENT:** The quotient is the answer in the division problem. In the next two lesson plans there will be explanations for quotient beads to help find answers, and Quotient Bingo to practice division facts. The **quotient** is the answer in the division problem.

**ASSIGNMENT:** Have students fill in the answers on the Practice Facts sheet or write it on the board and have them copy it and fill in the answers. This is a study sheet. Students can use the Base 10 Counting Chart, page protector and marker for help in finding an answer. For example,

$$5 \times 5 = ?$$

Circle five groups of five each. The last number circled is 25–the answer. Use the worksheets as homework.

**OPTIONAL:** Enlarge and laminate the Travel Folder for Squares and post it in the classroom so students can quiz themselves when they have free time.

**TAKE-HOME:** Send home the Travel Folder for Squares. (Students could make their own using construction paper or an index card.) Show students how to fold it in thirds vertically so that only one column shows on each section.

Students should memorize column one (on the left)–the perfect squares. Column two is used for practice. Students will learn to recite these facts in order. Students will recite them at the beginning of each class for several consecutive days until all in the class know them.

Column three is a compound flash card. A student will read the problem and give the correct answer. Turn back to column two if necessary.

Students should discuss with their parents where would be a good place to post the folder at home.

**FLASH CARDS:** Give each student a set of division flash cards. They should cut out the cards and begin studying them. Also, students could make their own flash cards using index cards. Put the problem on one side and the problem with the answer on the other side. This is a visual reinforcement to show which three numbers are related in division. This is better than having two different problems on each side of the same card.

**GAME:** Flash cards can be used in place of the question cards in Trivial Pursuit™. Play according to the rules.

# PERFECT SQUARES

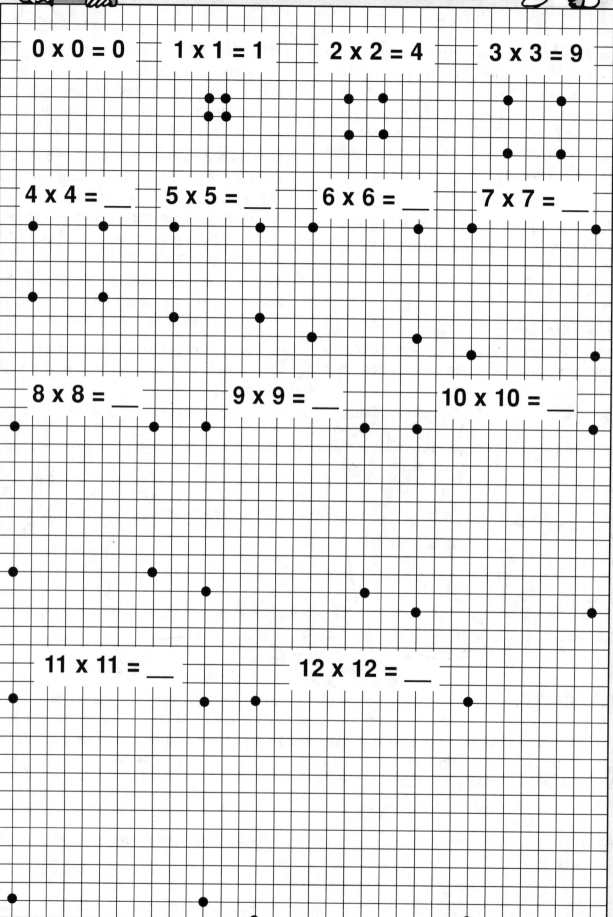

0 x 0 = 0　　1 x 1 = 1　　2 x 2 = 4　　3 x 3 = 9

4 x 4 = __　　5 x 5 = __　　6 x 6 = __　　7 x 7 = __

8 x 8 = __　　　9 x 9 = __　　　10 x 10 = __

11 x 11 = __　　　12 x 12 = __

**24**

| | | |
|---|---|---|
| $1 \overline{)\phantom{0} 0}$ | $2 \overline{)\phantom{0} 0}$ | $3 \overline{)\phantom{0} 0}$ |
| $4 \overline{)\phantom{0} 0}$ | $5 \overline{)\phantom{0} 0}$ | $6 \overline{)\phantom{0} 0}$ |
| $7 \overline{)\phantom{0} 0}$ | $8 \overline{)\phantom{0} 0}$ | $9 \overline{)\phantom{0} 0}$ |
| $10 \overline{)\phantom{0} 0}$ | $1 \overline{)\phantom{0} 1}$ | $1 \overline{)\phantom{0} 2}$ |
| $1 \overline{)\phantom{0} 3}$ | $1 \overline{)\phantom{0} 4}$ | $1 \overline{)\phantom{0} 5}$ |
| $1 \overline{)\phantom{0} 6}$ | $1 \overline{)\phantom{0} 7}$ | $1 \overline{)\phantom{0} 8}$ |
| $1 \overline{)\phantom{0} 9}$ | $1 \overline{)\phantom{0} 10}$ | $2 \overline{)\phantom{0} 2}$ |
| $2 \overline{)\phantom{0} 4}$ | $2 \overline{)\phantom{0} 6}$ | $2 \overline{)\phantom{0} 8}$ |

| | | |
|---|---|---|
| $3\overline{)0}^{\ 0}$ | $2\overline{)0}^{\ 0}$ | $1\overline{)0}^{\ 0}$ |
| $6\overline{)0}^{\ 0}$ | $5\overline{)0}^{\ 0}$ | $4\overline{)0}^{\ 0}$ |
| $9\overline{)0}^{\ 0}$ | $5\overline{)0}^{\ 0}$ | $7\overline{)0}^{\ 0}$ |
| $1\overline{)2}^{\ 2}$ | $1\overline{)1}^{\ 1}$ | $10\overline{)0}^{\ 0}$ |
| $1\overline{)5}^{\ 5}$ | $1\overline{)4}^{\ 4}$ | $1\overline{)3}^{\ 3}$ |
| $1\overline{)8}^{\ 8}$ | $1\overline{)7}^{\ 7}$ | $1\overline{)6}^{\ 6}$ |
| $2\overline{)2}^{\ 1}$ | $1\overline{)10}^{\ 10}$ | $1\overline{)9}^{\ 9}$ |
| $2\overline{)8}^{\ 4}$ | $2\overline{)6}^{\ 3}$ | $2\overline{)4}^{\ 2}$ |

$2\overline{)\ 10}$ | $2\overline{)\ 12}$ | $2\overline{)\ 14}$

$2\overline{)\ 16}$ | $2\overline{)\ 18}$ | $2\overline{)\ 20}$

$3\overline{)\ 3}$ | $3\overline{)\ 6}$ | $3\overline{)\ 9}$

$3\overline{)\ 12}$ | $3\overline{)\ 15}$ | $3\overline{)\ 18}$

$3\overline{)\ 21}$ | $3\overline{)\ 24}$ | $3\overline{)\ 27}$

$3\overline{)\ 30}$ | $4\overline{)\ 4}$ | $4\overline{)\ 8}$

$4\overline{)\ 12}$ | $4\overline{)\ 16}$ | $4\overline{)\ 20}$

$4\overline{)\ 24}$ | $4\overline{)\ 28}$ | $4\overline{)\ 32}$

| | | |
|---|---|---|
| $2\overline{)14}$ = 7 | $2\overline{)12}$ = 6 | $2\overline{)10}$ = 5 |
| $2\overline{)20}$ = 10 | $2\overline{)18}$ = 9 | $2\overline{)16}$ = 8 |
| $3\overline{)9}$ = 3 | $3\overline{)6}$ = 2 | $3\overline{)3}$ = 1 |
| $3\overline{)18}$ = 6 | $3\overline{)15}$ = 5 | $3\overline{)12}$ = 4 |
| $3\overline{)27}$ = 9 | $3\overline{)24}$ = 8 | $3\overline{)21}$ = 7 |
| $4\overline{)8}$ = 2 | $4\overline{)4}$ = 1 | $3\overline{)30}$ = 10 |
| $4\overline{)20}$ = 5 | $4\overline{)16}$ = 4 | $4\overline{)12}$ = 3 |
| $4\overline{)32}$ = 8 | $4\overline{)28}$ = 7 | $4\overline{)24}$ = 6 |

| | | |
|---|---|---|
| 4)‾36 | 4)‾40 | 5)‾5 |
| 5)‾10 | 5)‾15 | 5)‾20 |
| 5)‾25 | 5)‾30 | 5)‾35 |
| 5)‾40 | 5)‾45 | 5)‾50 |
| 6)‾6 | 6)‾12 | 6)‾18 |
| 6)‾24 | 6)‾30 | 6)‾36 |
| 6)‾42 | 6)‾48 | 6)‾54 |
| 6)‾60 | 7)‾7 | 7)‾14 |

| | | |
|---|---|---|
| $5 \overline{)\smash{\phantom{0}} 5}^{\,1}$ | $4 \overline{)\smash{\phantom{0}} 40}^{\,10}$ | $4 \overline{)\smash{\phantom{0}} 36}^{\,9}$ |
| $5 \overline{)\smash{\phantom{0}} 20}^{\,4}$ | $5 \overline{)\smash{\phantom{0}} 15}^{\,3}$ | $5 \overline{)\smash{\phantom{0}} 10}^{\,2}$ |
| $5 \overline{)\smash{\phantom{0}} 35}^{\,7}$ | $5 \overline{)\smash{\phantom{0}} 30}^{\,6}$ | $5 \overline{)\smash{\phantom{0}} 25}^{\,5}$ |
| $5 \overline{)\smash{\phantom{0}} 50}^{\,10}$ | $5 \overline{)\smash{\phantom{0}} 45}^{\,9}$ | $5 \overline{)\smash{\phantom{0}} 40}^{\,8}$ |
| $6 \overline{)\smash{\phantom{0}} 18}^{\,3}$ | $6 \overline{)\smash{\phantom{0}} 12}^{\,2}$ | $6 \overline{)\smash{\phantom{0}} 6}^{\,1}$ |
| $6 \overline{)\smash{\phantom{0}} 36}^{\,6}$ | $6 \overline{)\smash{\phantom{0}} 30}^{\,5}$ | $6 \overline{)\smash{\phantom{0}} 24}^{\,4}$ |
| $6 \overline{)\smash{\phantom{0}} 54}^{\,9}$ | $6 \overline{)\smash{\phantom{0}} 48}^{\,8}$ | $6 \overline{)\smash{\phantom{0}} 42}^{\,7}$ |
| $7 \overline{)\smash{\phantom{0}} 14}^{\,2}$ | $7 \overline{)\smash{\phantom{0}} 7}^{\,1}$ | $6 \overline{)\smash{\phantom{0}} 60}^{\,10}$ |

| | | |
|---|---|---|
| $7 \overline{)21}$ | $7 \overline{)28}$ | $7 \overline{)35}$ |
| $7 \overline{)42}$ | $7 \overline{)49}$ | $7 \overline{)56}$ |
| $7 \overline{)63}$ | $7 \overline{)70}$ | $8 \overline{)8}$ |
| $8 \overline{)16}$ | $8 \overline{)24}$ | $8 \overline{)32}$ |
| $8 \overline{)40}$ | $8 \overline{)48}$ | $8 \overline{)56}$ |
| $8 \overline{)64}$ | $8 \overline{)72}$ | $8 \overline{)80}$ |
| $9 \overline{)9}$ | $9 \overline{)18}$ | $9 \overline{)27}$ |
| $9 \overline{)36}$ | $9 \overline{)45}$ | $9 \overline{)54}$ |

| | | |
|---|---|---|
| $7 \overline{)\ 35}$ → 5 | $7 \overline{)\ 28}$ → 4 | $7 \overline{)\ 21}$ → 3 |
| $7 \overline{)\ 56}$ → 8 | $7 \overline{)\ 49}$ → 7 | $7 \overline{)\ 42}$ → 6 |
| $8 \overline{)\ 8}$ → 1 | $7 \overline{)\ 70}$ → 10 | $7 \overline{)\ 63}$ → 9 |
| $8 \overline{)\ 32}$ → 4 | $8 \overline{)\ 24}$ → 3 | $8 \overline{)\ 16}$ → 2 |
| $8 \overline{)\ 56}$ → 7 | $8 \overline{)\ 48}$ → 6 | $8 \overline{)\ 40}$ → 5 |
| $8 \overline{)\ 80}$ → 10 | $8 \overline{)\ 72}$ → 9 | $8 \overline{)\ 64}$ → 8 |
| $9 \overline{)\ 27}$ → 3 | $9 \overline{)\ 18}$ → 2 | $9 \overline{)\ 9}$ → 1 |
| $9 \overline{)\ 54}$ → 6 | $9 \overline{)\ 45}$ → 5 | $9 \overline{)\ 36}$ → 4 |

$9\overline{)63}$

$9\overline{)72}$

$9\overline{)81}$

$9\overline{)90}$

$10\overline{)10}$

$10\overline{)20}$

$10\overline{)30}$

$10\overline{)40}$

$10\overline{)50}$

$10\overline{)60}$

$10\overline{)70}$

$10\overline{)80}$

$10\overline{)90}$

$10\overline{)100}$

$$9\overline{)81} = 9$$

$$9\overline{)72} = 8$$

$$9\overline{)63} = 7$$

$$10\overline{)20} = 2$$

$$10\overline{)10} = 1$$

$$9\overline{)90} = 10$$

$$10\overline{)50} = 5$$

$$10\overline{)40} = 4$$

$$10\overline{)30} = 3$$

$$10\overline{)80} = 8$$

$$10\overline{)70} = 7$$

$$10\overline{)60} = 6$$

$$10\overline{)100} = 10$$

$$10\overline{)90} = 9$$

34

Name _____

# PRACTICE FACTS FOR SQUARES

1 x 1 = ___          ___ ÷ 1 = 1

2 x 2 = ___          ___ ÷ 2 = 2

3 x 3 = ___          ___ ÷ 3 = 3

4 x 4 = ___          ___ ÷ 4 = 4

5 x 5 = ___          ___ ÷ 5 = 5

6 x 6 = ___          ___ ÷ 6 = 6

7 x 7 = ___          ___ ÷ 7 = 7

8 x 8 = ___          ___ ÷ 8 = 8

9 x 9 = ___          ___ ÷ 9 = 9

10 x 10 = ___          ___ ÷ 10 = 10

# TRAVEL FOLDER FOR SQUARES

| | | |
|---|---|---|
| 1 | $1 \div 1 = 1$ | $1 \div 1$ |
| 4 | $4 \div 2 = 2$ | $4 \div 2$ |
| 9 | $9 \div 3 = 3$ | $9 \div 3$ |
| 16 | $16 \div 4 = 4$ | $16 \div 4$ |
| 25 | $25 \div 5 = 5$ | $25 \div 5$ |
| 36 | $36 \div 6 = 6$ | $36 \div 6$ |
| 49 | $49 \div 7 = 7$ | $49 \div 7$ |
| 64 | $64 \div 8 = 8$ | $64 \div 8$ |
| 81 | $81 \div 9 = 9$ | $81 \div 9$ |
| 100 | $100 \div 10 = 10$ | $100 \div 10$ |

# DIVIDING SQUARES

1.   $25 \div 5 =$ ___       2.   $81 \div 9 =$ ___

3.   $6\overline{)36}$       4.   $2\overline{)4}$

5.   $3\overline{)9}$       6.   $7\overline{)49}$

7.   $100 \div 10 =$ ___       8.   $8\overline{)64}$

9.   $1\overline{)1}$       10.   $4\overline{)16}$

11.   $9 \div 3 =$ ___       12.   $36 \div 6 =$ ___

13.   Ed bought 36 baseball cards.  He can put 6 cards in one page of his album.  How many pages will he need?

14.   There are 49 days until the end of school.  How many weeks is that?

15.   Jan has 25¢ in nickels.  How many nickels does she have?

## CHALLENGE:

a. $4\overline{)160}$    b. $4\overline{)1600}$    c. $3\overline{)90}$    d. $3\overline{)99}$    e. $3\overline{)900}$

f. $5\overline{)250}$    g. $5\overline{)255}$    h. $5\overline{)2500}$    i. $8\overline{)640}$    j. $9\overline{)810}$

**EXTRA CHALLENGE:**  On the back, correctly spell the three division terms. Ask your teacher to pronounce the three terms.

# SQUARES

## ACROSS

1. $4 \times 4 =$ _____

3. $6\overline{)\,?}$ (with 6 above)

6. $9 \times 4 =$ _____

9. $3 \times 4 =$ _____

10. $7\overline{)\,?}$ (with 7 above)

11. $5 \times 5 =$ _____

12. $9 \times 2 =$ _____

16. $4\overline{)\,?}$ (with 4 above)

18. $24 + 5 =$ _____

20. $58 + 3 =$ _____

22. $7 \times 11 =$ _____

23. $8 \times 9 =$ _____

25. $9 \times 6 =$ _____

28. $6 \times 8 =$ _____

29. $7 \times 8 =$ _____

| 1 | 2 | | | 3 | 4 | | 5 |
|---|---|---|---|---|---|---|---|
| **1** | **6** | | | | | | |
| | 6 | 7 | | 8 | | 9 | |
| | 10 | | | 11 | | | |
| 12 | 13 | | | 14 | | | 15 |
| | 16 | 17 | | | | 18 | |
| 19 | | 20 | 21 | | 22 | | |
| 23 | 24 | | 25 | 26 | | | 27 |
| | 28 | | | 29 | | | |

## DOWN

2. $7\overline{)\,?}$ (with 9 above)

9. $3 \times 5 =$ _____

17. $6 \times 11 =$ _____

24. $6 \times 4 =$ _____

3. $4 \times 8 =$ _____

13. $9\overline{)\,?}$ (with 9 above)

18. $23 + 4 =$ _____

26. $9 \times 5 =$ _____

5. $6 \times 7 =$ _____

14. $5\overline{)\,?}$ (with 9 above)

19. $3 \times 9 =$ _____

27. $3 \times 11 =$ _____

7. $8\overline{)\,?}$ (with 8 above)

15. $7\overline{)\,?}$ (with 7 above)

21. $3 \times 5 =$ _____

**CHALLENGE:** On the back, find the squares of 11, 12, 13, 14 and 15. (The square of 11 is $11^2$ or $11 \times 11$.)

**OBJECTIVE:** Dividing by 9. Students will learn division by nine. They will also practice with division facts in which the answer is nine. These we will refer to as the matching facts.

**MATERIALS:** Flash Cards (pages 25-34), Practice Facts for 9s (page 41), Travel Folder for 9s (page 42), Worksheets G and H (pages 43 and 44), Quotient Beads (page 40), Student's Math Phonics™ Progress Chart (page 45), Teacher's Math Phonics™ Progress Chart (page 46), Quiz Bowl (page 47)

**INTRODUCTION:** Have the class chant the left-hand column and the second column of the Travel Folder for Squares (page 36). Students can look at their own folder or the one on the wall if they need to, but in a day or two, they should be able to say this without help. If the class is having trouble saying the squares facts, the teacher could say the fact and the class could say the answer. They need to learn to say the facts in order and then at random. Have students stand up when they can say the facts without looking at a poster.

**DO:** Have the class review the facts for multiplying by nine from 9 x 1 to 9 x 10. Write the facts on the board and show the pattern in the answers:

9 x 1 = 9
9 x 2 = 18
9 x 3 = 27
9 x 4 = 36
9 x 5 = 45
9 x 6 = 54
9 x 7 = 63
9 x 8 = 72
9 x 9 = 81
9 x 10 = 90

Ask students what patterns they see.

1. Point out that for each answer, the sum of the numerals is nine.

   (1 + 8 = 9, 2 + 7 = 9, 3 + 6 = 9 and so on.)

2. Also, the numeral in the 10s place of the answer is one less than the number multiplied by nine. Example:

   9 x 3 = 27 (the 2 is one less than the 3)

   9 x 4 = 36 (the 3 is one less than the 4)

   9 x 5 = 45 (the 4 is one less than the 5)

3. Also, the numeral in the 1s place decreases and the numeral in the 10s place increases with each answer.

4. Finally, the answers can be put in reverse pairs—18 and 81, 27 and 72, 36 and 63, 45 and 54.

   Pick one of the facts and ask students to give the two division problems that use the same numbers.

| | | |
|---|---|---|
| 9 x 1 = 9 | 9 ÷ 9 = 1 | 9 ÷ 1 = 9 |
| 9 x 2 = 18 | 18 ÷ 9 = 2 | 18 ÷ 2 = 9 |
| 9 x 3 = 27 | 27 ÷ 9 = 3 | 27 ÷ 3 = 9 |
| 9 x 4 = 36 | 36 ÷ 9 = 4 | 36 ÷ 4 = 9 |
| 9 x 5 = 45 | 45 ÷ 9 = 5 | 45 ÷ 5 = 9 |
| 9 x 6 = 54 | 54 ÷ 9 = 6 | 54 ÷ 6 = 9 |
| 9 x 7 = 63 | 63 ÷ 9 = 7 | 63 ÷ 7 = 9 |
| 9 x 8 = 72 | 72 ÷ 9 = 8 | 72 ÷ 8 = 9 |
| 9 x 9 = 81 | 81 ÷ 9 = 9 | 81 ÷ 9 = 9 |
| 9 x 10 = 90 | 90 ÷ 9 = 10 | 90 ÷ 10 = 9 |

**DETOUR**

If necessary, use the Base 10 Counting Chart to demonstrate the division facts. Follow the steps in Lesson Plan 2.

Use the pattern in the nines to help think of answers. Look at these problems:

$$9\overline{)18}^{\,2} \qquad 9\overline{)27}^{\,3} \qquad 9\overline{)36}^{\,4} \qquad 9\overline{)45}^{\,5}$$

Ask the class if they can see a pattern here and make up a rule. Here's what they should come up with:

**RULE:** When dividing a two-digit number by nine, look at the number in the 10s place. Add one. That is the answer.

Here's another rule for 9s:

**RULE:** If the numerals of a number add up to nine, the number is divisible by nine.

**DETOUR**

**FLASH CARDS:** Have students cut out or make the 9 cards and put with the squares to study.

**IN CLASS:** Pass out the Practice Facts for 9s. Have students find answers on the counting chart if necessary. Write in the correct answers.

**TRAVEL FOLDER:** This travel folder has four columns—the first column is counting by nine, or multiples of nine, or numbers divisible by nine. The second contains all the 9s facts with answers. The third is 9s facts without answers, and the fourth is the matching facts without answers. All the answers to the fourth column are 9s.

**DETOUR**

**ASSIGNMENT:** Worksheets G and H.

**TAKE-HOME:** Travel Folder for 9s.

**QUOTIENT BEADS:** Here is a great way to make a division visual aid and recycle at the same time. For each set of quotient beads, you will need:

1. One shoelace or other heavy cord about 36" (1 m) long.

2. 100 barrel beads sold at most hobby stores. You could substitute colored wheel-shaped pasta, buttons with large holes, or other stringable items for the beads. You may have to adjust the length of the string.

3. Ten square plastic tabs used to close bread wrappers or twist ties.

Tie a large bead on one end of the shoelace as a stopper. This will not be used in the counting. String 10 beads of one color and then 10 of another color. Keep alternating colors until 100 beads have been strung. Tie on another large bead as a stopper. This will not be used in counting. These beads can be used to demonstrate division problems. Example: 48 ÷ 6 = ?

Count 48 of the counter beads and clip on a plastic tab. Now start at the beginning and count 6 beads and clip on a tab. Count 6 more and clip on a tab. Continue until you reach 48. Count the groups of 6—there are 8 groups. Thus: 48 ÷ 6 = 8

This can be used in place of the Base 10 Counting Chart in finding division answers.

**NOTE:** For Worksheet G, you might want to have a yardstick in the room so students can visualize how many feet are in a yard.

# PRACTICE FACTS FOR 9s

$9 \div 9 =$ ___

$18 \div 9 =$ ___

$27 \div 9 =$ ___

$36 \div 9 =$ ___

$45 \div 9 =$ ___

$54 \div 9 =$ ___

$63 \div 9 =$ ___

$72 \div 9 =$ ___

$81 \div 9 =$ ___

$90 \div 9 =$ ___

$9 \div 1 =$ ___

$18 \div 2 =$ ___

$27 \div 3 =$ ___

$36 \div 4 =$ ___

$45 \div 5 =$ ___

$54 \div 6 =$ ___

$63 \div 7 =$ ___

$72 \div 8 =$ ___

$81 \div 9 =$ ___

$90 \div 10 =$ ___

# TRAVEL FOLDER FOR 9s

| 9 | 9 ÷ 9 = 1 | 9 ÷ 9 | 9 ÷ 1 |
|---|---|---|---|
| 18 | 18 ÷ 9 = 2 | 18 ÷ 9 | 18 ÷ 2 |
| 27 | 27 ÷ 9 = 3 | 27 ÷ 9 | 27 ÷ 3 |
| 36 | 36 ÷ 9 = 4 | 36 ÷ 9 | 36 ÷ 4 |
| 45 | 45 ÷ 9 = 5 | 45 ÷ 9 | 45 ÷ 5 |
| 54 | 54 ÷ 9 = 6 | 54 ÷ 9 | 54 ÷ 6 |
| 63 | 63 ÷ 9 = 7 | 63 ÷ 9 | 63 ÷ 7 |
| 72 | 72 ÷ 9 = 8 | 72 ÷ 9 | 72 ÷ 8 |
| 81 | 81 ÷ 9 = 9 | 81 ÷ 9 | 81 ÷ 9 |
| 90 | 90 ÷ 9 = 10 | 90 ÷ 9 | 90 ÷ 10 |

# DIVIDING BY 9

1. Name pairs of whole numbers you can add to equal nine: 9 + 0, 8 + 1, ____, ____, ____, ____, ____, ____, 1 + 8

2. Circle the numbers that are divisible by nine: 3, 18, 12, 29, 36, 90, 81, 54, 46, 73, 27, 45, 63

Find the answers.

3. **45 ÷ 9 = ___**       4. **27 ÷ 9 = ___**

5. **81 ÷ 9 = ___**       6. **54 ÷ 6 = ___**

7. **18 ÷ 9 = ___**       8. **36 ÷ 9 = ___**

9. **72 ÷ 8 = ___**       10. **36 ÷ 4 = ___**

11. **45 ÷ 5 = ___**      12. **72 ÷ 9 = ___**

13. **9)‾54‾**            14. **1)‾9‾**

15. **9)‾18‾**            16. **9)‾9‾**

17. **7)‾63‾**            18. **2)‾18‾**

19. Twenty-seven kids signed up for the baseball team. With 9 on a team, how many teams can they make?

**CHALLENGE:** Carla is putting up a wallpaper border. She measured and found that she needs 12 yards. How many feet does she need? If all walls are the same size, what is the length of one wall?

# DIVIDING BY 9 OR SQUARES

Count by 9s: 9, 18, ____, ____, ____, 54, ____, ____, ____, 90

Find the answers.

1. **90 ÷ 9 = ___**

2. **63 ÷ 7 = ___**

3. **18 ÷ 2 = ___**

4. **36 ÷ 9 = ___**

5. **45 ÷ 5 = ___**

6. **72 ÷ 9 = ___**

7. **9 ÷ 1 = ___**

8. **27 ÷ 3 = ___**

9. **81 ÷ 9 = ___**

10. **54 ÷ 9 = ___**

11. **5)‾25‾**

12. **8)‾64‾**

13. **10)‾100‾**

14. **6)‾36‾**

15. **7)‾49‾**

16. **3)‾9‾**

17. **2)‾4‾**

18. **4)‾36‾**

19. **9)‾27‾**

20. **6)‾54‾**

21. Margaret is making a design with bricks in her garden. She has 36 bricks. If she puts 6 bricks in each row, how many rows would she have?

22. If Margaret used 4 bricks in each row, how many rows would she have?

**CHALLENGE:**
   a. If Margaret used 3 bricks in a row, how many rows would she have?
   b. On the back of this page, write the multiples of 9 from 9 to 198.

Name _____

# TUDENT'S MATH PHONICS™ PROGRESS CHART

| | Say facts in order | Say facts not in order | **Practice Facts** How many right? | **Worksheet** How many right? |
|---|---|---|---|---|
| Squares | | | | |
| 9s | | | | |
| 2s | | | | |
| 4s | | | | |
| 8s | | | | |
| 5s | | | | |
| 10s | | | | |
| 3s | | | | |
| 6s | | | | |
| 7s | | | | |
| Assessment | X | X | X | X |

Have a parent or classmate sign these spaces when you can say them correctly.

| Name | Squares | 9s | 2s | 4s | 8s | 5s | 10s | 3s | 6s | 7s | Assessment |
|---|---|---|---|---|---|---|---|---|---|---|---|
|  |  |  |  |  |  |  |  |  |  |  |  |
|  |  |  |  |  |  |  |  |  |  |  |  |
|  |  |  |  |  |  |  |  |  |  |  |  |
|  |  |  |  |  |  |  |  |  |  |  |  |
|  |  |  |  |  |  |  |  |  |  |  |  |
|  |  |  |  |  |  |  |  |  |  |  |  |
|  |  |  |  |  |  |  |  |  |  |  |  |
|  |  |  |  |  |  |  |  |  |  |  |  |
|  |  |  |  |  |  |  |  |  |  |  |  |
|  |  |  |  |  |  |  |  |  |  |  |  |
|  |  |  |  |  |  |  |  |  |  |  |  |
|  |  |  |  |  |  |  |  |  |  |  |  |
|  |  |  |  |  |  |  |  |  |  |  |  |
|  |  |  |  |  |  |  |  |  |  |  |  |
|  |  |  |  |  |  |  |  |  |  |  |  |
|  |  |  |  |  |  |  |  |  |  |  |  |
|  |  |  |  |  |  |  |  |  |  |  |  |
|  |  |  |  |  |  |  |  |  |  |  |  |

Write the date when the student has mastered peach group.

# QUIZ BOWL

Set aside 5 or 10 minutes at the end of each day for a classroom quiz bowl.

*1.* Divide the class into two teams.

*2.* Use math flash cards for questions.

*3.* Keep index cards at hand. When the quicker students finish their work early, have them write a question from another subject on an index card.* Check to be sure that they are appropriate. Use these as well as the flash cards.

*4.* Keep track of points. Give a small prize at the end of the week—perhaps gum or a pencil for each member of the winning team. A free homework pass is a good prize, but don't use that very often. Parents could be asked to donate prizes.

*Other students could take index cards home to write questions. Have students put names on cards and thank them for the question when it is used.

# LESSON PLAN 5

**OBJECTIVE:** Dividing by 2. Students will learn to divide by two. They will also learn division facts in which the answer is two. They will learn how to use zero in division.

**MATERIALS:** Practice Facts for 2s (page 50); Travel Folder for 2s (page 51); Worksheets I and J (pages 52 and 53); Mid-Unit Assessment for Squares, 9s and 2s (pages 54 and 55); Base 10 Counting Chart (page 95)

**INTRODUCTION:** Have students chant the squares division facts in order without looking at any charts. If students are having trouble with this, have them chant the squares alone–1, 4, 9, 16, 25, 36, 49, 64, 81, 100–and then the facts.

Have students chant the 9s division facts in order. If this is difficult, then begin by chanting the multiples of nine first: 9, 18, 27, 36, 45, 54, 63, 72, 81, 90.

After students have learned to say a group of facts correctly, the teacher should call out facts at random and ask for the answer. This, of course, is the goal–to be able to think of one fact without having to go through the whole list.

**REVIEW:** Write the 2s multiplication facts from 2 x 1 to 2 x 10 on the board and ask the class for the answers. Ask students to tell you the related division facts for each one.

For example: 2 x 3 = 6   6 ÷ 3 = 2   6 ÷ 2 = 3

(See page 9 for a list of the division facts.)

Ask the class if they remember how to tell if a number is an even number.

**RULE:** All even numbers end in 0, 2, 4, 6 or 8. All even numbers are divisible by two.

**NOTE:** Use the Base 10 Counting Chart if necessary for this next section.

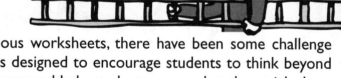

**ADVANCED DIVISION:** In some of the previous worksheets, there have been some challenge problems which have used larger numbers. This was designed to encourage students to think beyond one or two digits. Spend a little more time on this now, and help students grasp what they might have gotten right by guessing on the challenge problems.

Look at these problems:  6 ÷ 2 = 3   60 ÷ 2 = ?

Students will probably guess the answer is 30, but how do we know that is right?

If necessary, circle groups of two on the Base 10 Counting Chart ending with 60. Then count the groups to find the answer–30. Another method is to draw 6 boxes on the board. Each box represents 10. If you divide them into two groups, there are three boxes in each group–30 in each group. For 600 ÷ 2, each box would have 100 and dividing by 2 would give 300 in each group. Students need to know that for these types of problems, they just need to divide each numeral by 2. So for 666 ÷ 2, they divide each numeral and the answer is 333.

This makes sense because 333 + 333 = 666.

Try a few more examples.  888 ÷ 2 = 444 since each of the 8s is divisible by 2. Also 444 + 444 = 888.

How about 4,684 ÷ 2 = ?

Divide each of the numerals by 2. The answer is 2,342. Check by adding 2,342 + 2,342 = 4,684.

**CLASSROOM ACTIVITY:** Let students work in pairs. Have them make up division problems using 2, 4, 6 or 8 and dividing by 2. Check by adding.

**ZERO IN DIVISION:** Zero divided by any number always equals zero. This is logical. If I have no money and I share equally with a friend, we both have no money. If I share with nine friends, we all have no money. Therefore: $0 \div 2 = 0$, $0 \div 3 = 0$, $0 \div 4 = 0$ and so on.

**RULE:** Zero divided by any number always equals zero. The explanation makes more sense if this comes right after the Zero in the Division section.

**GAMES:** A RACKO™ game can be used to drill division facts. If students are studying the 2s division facts, take out all the even numbers from the RACKO™ cards. Turn up one card—let's say the 14. The student must use this to make a 2s division fact and then give the answer. $14 \div 2 = 7$. They could also give the matching fact—$14 \div 7 = 2$.

For the 9s, you would use the cards with numbers divisible by nine. Do the same for any group.

**QUIZZES:** For a quick check on how students are progressing, use a T-table quiz. An example is given on the right. Each student makes the T chart on paper. If the quiz is over the 9s, they write ÷ 9 at the top. The teacher reads off the numbers divisible by nine in random order and students write the numbers in the left-hand column. Answers are written in the right-hand column.

| ÷ | 9 |
|---|---|
| 63 | |
| 45 | |
| 9 | |
| 18 | |
| 36 | |
| 27 | |
| 54 | |
| 90 | |
| 81 | |
| 72 | |

**OPTIONAL:** Study another unit such as measurement so that slower students have time to catch up on memory work. Send home Note 2 on page 56.

**DIVIDING BY ZERO:** This is another matter. It seems that we should be able to divide by zero, but here's what happens when we try to do that. In division problems, the divisor times the quotient should give us the dividend. For example:

$$9\overline{)18} = 2$$

When we try to do this with zeros, we run into trouble. Look at this problem using zero:

$$0\overline{)9}$$

There is no number that you can multiply times zero to get 9.

*Division by zero is said to be undefined.*

Zero could be a part of the divisor—for example, we could divide by 10 which has a zero in it. But the entire divisor can't be zero.

**ASSIGNMENT:** Use Practice Facts, Travel Folders, Worksheets and flash cards as described in previous lessons.

Use a Mid-Unit Assessment to check students' progress.

**LAST BLAST:** One last suggestion for teaching the 2s—relate them to the doubles in addition. Here is an example:

$$8 + 8 = 16 \qquad 16 \div 2 = 8$$

If students have the addition doubles well memorized, that will help them in dividing by two.

# PRACTICE FACTS FOR 2s

| | |
|---|---|
| 2 ÷ 2 = ___ | 2 ÷ 1 = ___ |
| 4 ÷ 2 = ___ | 4 ÷ 2 = ___ |
| 6 ÷ 2 = ___ | 6 ÷ 3 = ___ |
| 8 ÷ 2 = ___ | 8 ÷ 4 = ___ |
| 10 ÷ 2 = ___ | 10 ÷ 5 = ___ |
| 12 ÷ 2 = ___ | 12 ÷ 6 = ___ |
| 14 ÷ 2 = ___ | 14 ÷ 7 = ___ |
| 16 ÷ 2 = ___ | 16 ÷ 8 = ___ |
| 18 ÷ 2 = ___ | 18 ÷ 9 = ___ |
| 20 ÷ 2 = ___ | 20 ÷ 10 = ___ |

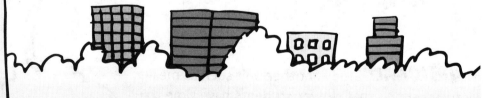

Name _____

# TRAVEL FOLDER FOR 2s

| | | |
|---|---|---|
| 2 ÷ 2 = 1 | 2 ÷ 2 | 1)2̄ |
| 4 ÷ 2 = 2 | 4 ÷ 2 | 2)4̄ |
| 6 ÷ 2 = 3 | 6 ÷ 2 | 3)6̄ |
| 8 ÷ 2 = 4 | 8 ÷ 2 | 4)8̄ |
| 10 ÷ 2 = 5 | 10 ÷ 2 | 5)1̄0̄ |
| 12 ÷ 2 = 6 | 12 ÷ 2 | 6)1̄2̄ |
| 14 ÷ 2 = 7 | 14 ÷ 2 | 7)1̄4̄ |
| 16 ÷ 2 = 8 | 16 ÷ 2 | 8)1̄6̄ |
| 18 ÷ 2 = 9 | 18 ÷ 2 | 9)1̄8̄ |
| 20 ÷ 2 = 10 | 20 ÷ 2 | 10)2̄0̄ |

**51**

Name _____

# DIVIDING BY 2

1. $8 \div 2 =$ ___

2. $4 \div 2 =$ ___

3. $6 \div 2 =$ ___

4. $12 \div 2 =$ ___

5. $18 \div 2 =$ ___

6. $20 \div 2 =$ ___

7. $2 \div 2 =$ ___

8. $2 \overline{)0}$

9. $3 \overline{)0}$

10. $2 \overline{)14}$

11. $2 \overline{)16}$

12. $2 \overline{)20}$

13. $8 \overline{)16}$

14. $7 \overline{)14}$

15. $4 \overline{)8}$

16. $6 \overline{)12}$

17. $5 \overline{)0}$

18. $3 \overline{)6}$

19. $2 \overline{)18}$

20. $2 \overline{)14}$

## ADVANCED DIVISION

21. $2 \overline{)24}$

22. $2 \overline{)66}$

23. $2 \overline{)88}$

24. $2 \overline{)684}$

25. $2 \overline{)48}$

26. $2 \overline{)868}$

27. $2 \overline{)6,248}$

28. $2 \overline{)8,682}$

**CHALLENGE:** A new math process has been invented. It is called the box process (■).
Here are some problems using this process: 2 ■ = 6, 3 ■ = 9, 4 ■ = 12.
Can you find the answer to these problems: 5 ■ = ___ , 6 ■ = ___ . On the back of this page,
describe how this process works.

Name _____

# DIVIDING BY 9s AND 2s

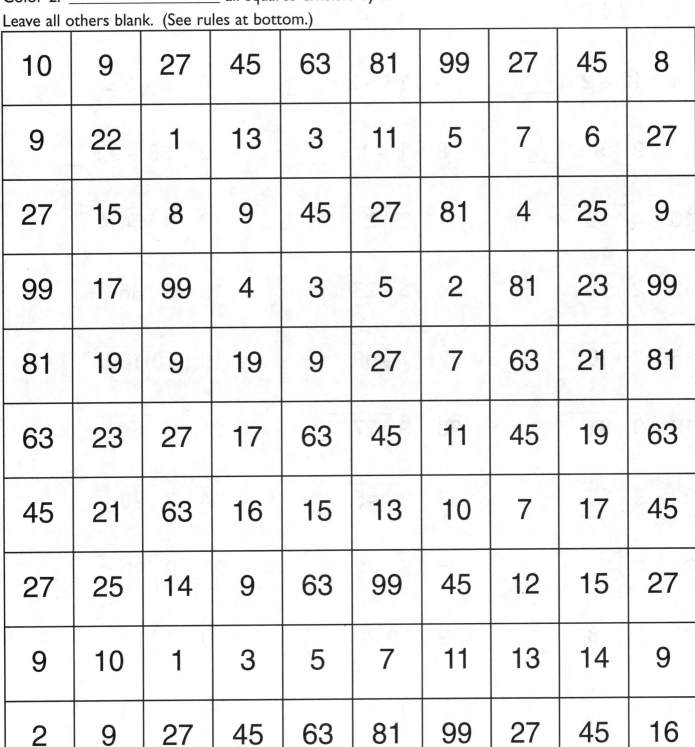

Choose two colors.

Color 1: _____ all squares divisible by 9.

Color 2: _____ all squares divisible by 2.

Leave all others blank. (See rules at bottom.)

| 10 | 9 | 27 | 45 | 63 | 81 | 99 | 27 | 45 | 8 |
|---|---|---|---|---|---|---|---|---|---|
| 9 | 22 | 1 | 13 | 3 | 11 | 5 | 7 | 6 | 27 |
| 27 | 15 | 8 | 9 | 45 | 27 | 81 | 4 | 25 | 9 |
| 99 | 17 | 99 | 4 | 3 | 5 | 2 | 81 | 23 | 99 |
| 81 | 19 | 9 | 19 | 9 | 27 | 7 | 63 | 21 | 81 |
| 63 | 23 | 27 | 17 | 63 | 45 | 11 | 45 | 19 | 63 |
| 45 | 21 | 63 | 16 | 15 | 13 | 10 | 7 | 17 | 45 |
| 27 | 25 | 14 | 9 | 63 | 99 | 45 | 12 | 15 | 27 |
| 9 | 10 | 1 | 3 | 5 | 7 | 11 | 13 | 14 | 9 |
| 2 | 9 | 27 | 45 | 63 | 81 | 99 | 27 | 45 | 16 |

**RULE:** If the numerals in a number add up to 9, the number is divisible by 9.

**RULE:** If a number ends in 0, 2, 4, 6 or 8, it is divisible by 2.

53

# MID-UNIT ASSESSMENT FOR SQUARES, 9s AND 2s

1.  $18 \div 9 =$ _____

2.  $4 \div 2 =$ _____

3.  $6 \div 2 =$ _____

4.  $12 \div 2 =$ _____

5.  $16 \div 2 =$ _____

6.  $9 \div 3 =$ _____

7.  $9 \div 9 =$ _____

8.  $1 \div 1 =$ _____

9.  $36 \div 9 =$ _____

10. $4\,\overline{)16}$

11. $2\,\overline{)2}$

12. $9\,\overline{)54}$

13. $2\,\overline{)14}$

14. $5\,\overline{)25}$

15. $6\,\overline{)36}$

16. $2\,\overline{)10}$

17. $7\,\overline{)49}$

18. $10\,\overline{)100}$

19. $9\,\overline{)81}$

20. $9\,\overline{)27}$

21. $8\,\overline{)64}$

22. $9\,\overline{)63}$

23. $9\,\overline{)45}$

24. $2\,\overline{)20}$

25. $2\,\overline{)8}$

26. $9\,\overline{)72}$

27. $9\,\overline{)90}$

28. $2\,\overline{)18}$

29. $10\,\overline{)20}$

30. $7\,\overline{)14}$

31. $1\,\overline{)9}$

32. $3\,\overline{)6}$

33. $5\,\overline{)10}$

34. $7\,\overline{)63}$

35. $1\,\overline{)2}$

36. $3\,\overline{)27}$

# MID-UNIT ASSESSMENT FOR SQUARES, 9s AND 2s

37. $10\overline{)90}$ 　　　38. $5\overline{)45}$ 　　　39. $9\overline{)54}$

40. $6\overline{)12}$ 　　　41. $8\overline{)16}$ 　　　42. $4\overline{)36}$

43. $2\overline{)10}$ 　　　44. $6\overline{)54}$ 　　　45. $8\overline{)72}$

46. $4\overline{)8}$ 　　　47. $9\overline{)54}$ 　　　48. $8\overline{)64}$

49. The Tyler Road School is holding a Fun Night to raise money for the homeless shelter. Nine classrooms will take part. Thirty-six parents have agreed to help. How many parents should help in each room?

50. There are 18 games to be played at Fun Night. How many games should be run by each of the 9 classes?

## CHALLENGE:

a. Six of the games will have two-liter bottles of cola as prizes. Families have donated 360 bottles of cola. How many should go to each of the 6 games?

b. Three of the games will use candy as prizes. If 270 boxes of candy have been given, how many boxes should be used for each game?

c. Fun Night tickets are printed with 6 tickets in each row and 9 rows of tickets on each page. One hundred pages of tickets have been printed. How many tickets will go to each of the 9 classes?

d. Nine businesses each donated 4 large pizzas. What is the total number of large pizzas? Large pizzas will be given away at 6 different times during Fun Night. How many pizzas will be given away at each time?

**Dear Parents,**

Our class has been working on division facts for two weeks. Thank you very much for the help you have given

at home. Your child has mastered these groups of facts: _____

Your child needs to learn these facts as soon as possible: _____

For the next two weeks, we will be studying a unit on _____. During that time, your child
still needs to review and practice these first groups. Use the flash cards and games. Please keep them in the
pocket folder and help your child with them at least two or three times a week.

After we finish the unit above, we will return to division
for another two-week unit. Then later in the year, we will
have periodic reviews. I want the children to practice at
home at least once a week for the rest of the year. The
facts are extremely important for the children to master
before they go on to new math material.

Once again, thank you for helping at home.

Sincerely,

**Dear Parents,**

We have now finished our last two weeks of *Math Phonics*™*–Division*. Your child still needs to spend some more

time on these groups: _____

We will begin a unit on _____ soon, so, it is very important that your child keep practicing
those groups mentioned above.

For a fun review, use the Division Facts
Chart. Ask your child the facts one at a time
and place a penny over each correct answer,
pennies will overlap slightly. Let your child
keep the pennies.

Keep these *Math Phonics*™ materials for
review in the future.

Sincerely,

# LESSON PLAN 6

**OBJECTIVE:** Dividing by 4 and 8. Students will learn to divide by four and by eight. They will also learn the matching facts in which four is the answer and in which eight is the answer.

**MATERIALS:** page protectors and markers, if needed; Flash Cards (pages 25-34); Practice Facts for 4s (page 58); Travel Folder for 4s (pages 59); Practice Facts for 8s (page 62); Travel Folder for 8s (page 63); Worksheets K, L, M and N (pages 60, 61, 64 and 65); Base 10 Counting Chart (page 95)

**INTRODUCTION:** Have the class chant the squares division facts if necessary. Omit them if all in the class have them memorized.

Have students chant division facts for nine and the division facts for two.

**FLASH CARDS:** Cut out the flash cards for dividing by four, and also for the facts in which the answers are four. Add these to the groups which the students have been studying in previous lessons.

**NOTE:** Have a parent volunteer come to class to listen to students count by 4s and count by 8s. Also, the students could pair off into math "study buddies" and listen to each other.

**TAKE-HOME:** Use Practice Facts sheets, Travel Folders and Worksheets as needed. One of the 8s facts that frequently gives students a problem is this:

7 x 8 = 56    56 ÷ 8 = 7    56 ÷ 7 = 8

Help your students by pointing out this mnemonic device:

5, 6, 7, 8
56 = 7 x 8
56 ÷ 7 = 8

**REVIEW:** Ask the class to give the 4s multiplication facts and write them in order on the board. Before looking at division, take a look at the pattern in the answers.

4,    8,    12,    16,    20,
24,    28,    32,    36,    40

This group consists of every other even number. Students should practice counting by fours until this can be done very quickly. These numbers are all divisible by four. All numbers evenly divisible by four must be even numbers.

Now ask the class for the two division problems for each multiplication problem:

4 x 1 = 4      4 ÷ 1 = 4      4 ÷ 4 = 1
4 x 2 = 8      8 ÷ 2 = 4      8 ÷ 4 = 2
4 x 3 = 12    12 ÷ 3 = 4    12 ÷ 4 = 3 and so on.

Ask students which of these have already been learned. They should say 16 ÷ 4 was learned with the squares, 8 ÷ 4 was learned with the 2s, 8 ÷ 2 was learned with the 2s and 36 ÷ 9 and 36 ÷ 4 were learned with the 9s.

**DIVIDING BY 8:** Use the above procedure. Point out the pattern in the 1s place—

8,    16,    24,    32,    40,
48,    56,    64,    72,    80

# PRACTICE FACTS FOR 4s

| | |
|---|---|
| 4 ÷ 4 = ___ | 4 ÷ 1 = ___ |
| 8 ÷ 4 = ___ | 8 ÷ 2 = ___ |
| 12 ÷ 4 = ___ | 12 ÷ 3 = ___ |
| 16 ÷ 4 = ___ | 16 ÷ 4 = ___ |
| 20 ÷ 4 = ___ | 20 ÷ 5 = ___ |
| 24 ÷ 4 = ___ | 24 ÷ 6 = ___ |
| 28 ÷ 4 = ___ | 28 ÷ 7 = ___ |
| 32 ÷ 4 = ___ | 32 ÷ 8 = ___ |
| 36 ÷ 4 = ___ | 36 ÷ 9 = ___ |
| 40 ÷ 4 = ___ | 40 ÷ 10 = ___ |

# TRAVEL FOLDER FOR 4s

| 4  | 4 ÷ 4 = 1   | 4 ÷ 4  | 4 ÷ 1  |
|----|-------------|--------|--------|
| 8  | 8 ÷ 4 = 2   | 8 ÷ 4  | 8 ÷ 2  |
| 12 | 12 ÷ 4 = 3  | 12 ÷ 4 | 12 ÷ 3 |
| 16 | 16 ÷ 4 = 4  | 16 ÷ 4 | 16 ÷ 4 |
| 20 | 20 ÷ 4 = 5  | 20 ÷ 4 | 20 ÷ 5 |
| 24 | 24 ÷ 4 = 6  | 24 ÷ 4 | 24 ÷ 6 |
| 28 | 28 ÷ 4 = 7  | 28 ÷ 4 | 28 ÷ 7 |
| 32 | 32 ÷ 4 = 8  | 32 ÷ 4 | 32 ÷ 8 |
| 36 | 36 ÷ 4 = 9  | 36 ÷ 4 | 36 ÷ 9 |
| 40 | 40 ÷ 4 = 10 | 40 ÷ 4 | 40 ÷ 10 |

Name _____

# DIVIDING BY 4

1. Write the numbers that are divisible by four:

   4, 8, ____, ____, ____, ____, ____, ____, ____, 40

2. 3)12      3. 4)24      4. 6)24      5. 4)8

6. 1)4      7. 4)28      8. 4)4      9. 4)12

10. 2)8      11. 8)32      12. 4)32      13. 4)16

14. 9)36      15. 4)20      16. 4)40      17. 7)28

18. 10)40      19. 5)20      20. 4)36

21. On the back of this page, write all the numbers divisible by four (every fourth number) from 4 to 100.

22. Jim has a dime collection. He wants to turn in his four quarters for dimes. How many dimes will he get?

**CHALLENGE:** Ten vans are taking students from Mayfield School to the state fair. Each van holds 10 students. Each student has 10 dollars to spend. How much money do the students have in all?

# DIVIDING BY 4

1. Place each number in the correct column. Some numbers may be placed in more than one column.

2, 4, 6, 8, 9, 12, 14, 16, 18, 20, 24, 27, 28, 32, 36, 40, 45

| Divisible by 9 | Divisible by 2 | Divisible by 4 |
|---|---|---|
| | | |

2. The coach tells John that he scored a total of 12 runs in the first 4 baseball games. John's mother says he scored the same number of runs in each game. How many runs did he have in each game?

3. Can you find this number? It is divisible by nine. It is a perfect square. It is *not* 81! What is the number?

**CHALLENGE:** A sticker is 1" on each side. If a page of stickers is 6 stickers wide and 8 stickers long, how many square inches does it cover?

# PRACTICE FACTS FOR 8s

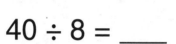

8 ÷ 8 = ___          8 ÷ 1 = ___

16 ÷ 8 = ___          16 ÷ 2 = ___

24 ÷ 8 = ___          24 ÷ 3 = ___

32 ÷ 8 = ___          32 ÷ 4 = ___

40 ÷ 8 = ___          40 ÷ 5 = ___

48 ÷ 8 = ___          48 ÷ 6 = ___

56 ÷ 8 = ___          56 ÷ 7 = ___

64 ÷ 8 = ___          64 ÷ 8 = ___

72 ÷ 8 = ___          72 ÷ 9 = ___

80 ÷ 8 = ___          80 ÷ 10 = ___

# TRAVEL FOLDER FOR 8s

| | | | |
|---|---|---|---|
| 8 | 8 ÷ 8 = 1 | 8 ÷ 8 | 8 ÷ 1 |
| 16 | 16 ÷ 8 = 2 | 16 ÷ 8 | 16 ÷ 2 |
| 24 | 24 ÷ 8 = 3 | 24 ÷ 8 | 24 ÷ 3 |
| 32 | 32 ÷ 8 = 4 | 32 ÷ 8 | 32 ÷ 4 |
| 40 | 40 ÷ 8 = 5 | 40 ÷ 8 | 40 ÷ 5 |
| 48 | 48 ÷ 8 = 6 | 48 ÷ 8 | 48 ÷ 6 |
| 56 | 56 ÷ 8 = 7 | 56 ÷ 8 | 56 ÷ 7 |
| 64 | 64 ÷ 8 = 8 | 64 ÷ 8 | 64 ÷ 8 |
| 72 | 72 ÷ 8 = 9 | 72 ÷ 8 | 72 ÷ 9 |
| 80 | 80 ÷ 8 = 10 | 80 ÷ 8 | 80 ÷ 10 |

# DIVIDING BY 8

1. 2$\overline{)16}$    2. 8$\overline{)24}$    3. 3$\overline{)24}$    4. 8$\overline{)80}$

5. 8$\overline{)48}$    6. 5$\overline{)40}$    7. 6$\overline{)48}$    8. 8$\overline{)32}$

9. 8$\overline{)8}$    10. 8$\overline{)56}$    11. 8$\overline{)64}$    12. 8$\overline{)72}$

13. 8$\overline{)16}$    14. 8$\overline{)64}$    15. 8$\overline{)72}$    16. 8$\overline{)32}$

17. 8$\overline{)80}$    18. 1$\overline{)8}$    19. 7$\overline{)56}$    20. 8$\overline{)40}$

**CHALLENGE:** Use a Base 10 Counting Chart. Circle each number that is divisible by eight. Draw a box around each number that is divisible by four. Put an X on each number that is divisible by nine.

a. List all the numbers divisible by eight and also by four.
b. List all the numbers divisible by four and also by nine.
c. List all the numbers divisible by nine and also by eight.

# TREASURE HUNT

There are two paths to the treasure. Each division bracket is a doorway, and you must find each path through doors that have the same answer. (Hint: Answer all the problems first and then find the two paths.)

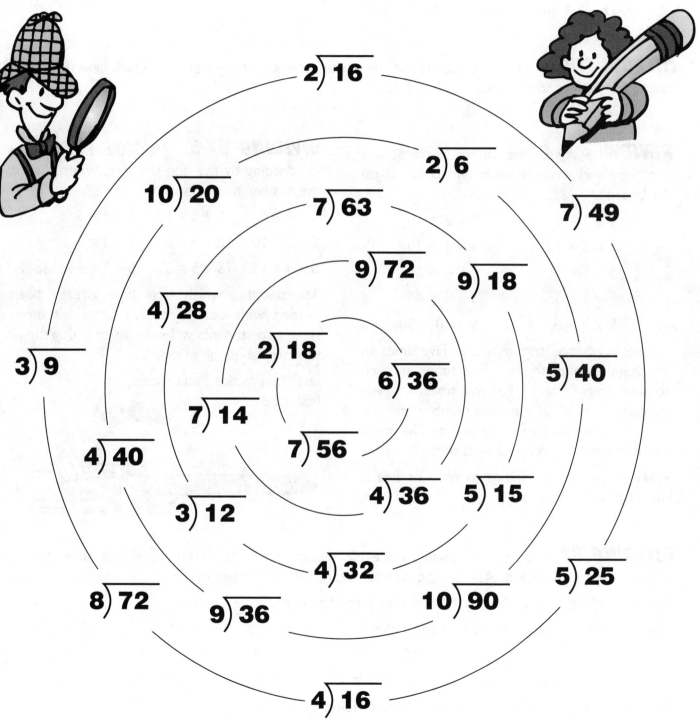

**OBJECTIVE:** Dividing by 5 and 10. Students will learn division facts for five and division facts for 10. They will also learn matching facts for five and ten.

**MATERIALS:** Flash Cards (pages 25-34); Quotient Bingo (page 68); Practice Facts for 5s (page 69); Travel Folder for 5s (page 70); Practice Facts for 10s (page 72); Travel Folder for 10s (page 73); Worksheets O, P and Q (pages 71, 74 and 75)

**INTRODUCTION:** Have the class chant any of the previously taught groups which have not been mastered—perfect squares, 9s, 5s, 4s and 8s.

**REVIEW:** Ask students for the 5s multiplication facts and write them in two columns on the board.

| | |
|---|---|
| 5 x 1 = 5 | 5 x 2 = 10 |
| 5 x 3 = 15 | 5 x 4 = 20 |
| 5 x 5 = 25 | 5 x 6 = 30 |
| 5 x 7 = 35 | 5 x 8 = 40 |
| 5 x 9 = 45 | 5 x 10 = 50 |

Ask them what pattern they see. Five times an odd number ends in five. Five times an even number ends in zero. For five times an even number, take half of the even number and put it in the 10s place of the answer. The most important rule to remember is this:

**RULE:** Any number ending in zero or five is always divisible by five.

**DIVIDING BY 5:** Write the division facts for dividing by five and the facts where five is the answer on the board:

| | | |
|---|---|---|
| 5 x 1 = 5 | 5 ÷ 5 = 1 | 5 ÷ 1 = 5 |
| 5 x 2 = 10 | 10 ÷ 5 = 2 | 10 ÷ 2 = 5 |
| 5 x 3 = 15 | 15 ÷ 5 = 3 | 15 ÷ 3 = 5 and so on. |

Ask students which facts have already been learned with other groups. Cross off those groups so students will see that they don't have to worry about all of them.

Use the Practice Facts sheets, Travel Folders and flash cards.

**DIVIDING BY 10:** Ask the class for the 10s multiplication facts from 10 x 1 to 10 x 10 and write them on the board. Ask for the rule for multiplying a number by 10.

**RULE:** To multiply a number by 10, add a zero to the right of the number.

Now ask the students for the corresponding division facts.

| | | |
|---|---|---|
| 10 x 1 = 10 | 10 ÷ 10 = 1 | 10 ÷ 1 = 10 |
| 10 x 2 = 20 | 20 ÷ 10 = 2 | 20 ÷ 2 = 10 and so on. |

Ask the class if they can make up a rule for dividing by 10.

**RULE:** If a number ends in zero, it is divisible by 10. To divide by 10, remove the zero.

Ask the class to name all the 10s facts that have been learned in previous lessons. Cross them off.

**OPTIONAL:** If you used *Math Phonics™–Multiplication* to teach the multiplication facts, students should know the rule for multiplying a number by 100. If not, here is an example:

**Example:** Draw several squares on the board. These are boxes of beads on sale at the hobby shop. There are 100 beads in each box. If you buy 3 boxes of beads, how many beads will you have?

$$3 \times 100 = ?$$

We can find the answer by adding 100 + 100 + 100 = 300. The shortcut would be to add two zeros to the right of the three.

$$3 \times 100 = 300$$

**RULE:** To multiply a number by 100, add two zeros to the right of the number.

Now look at the multiplication problem with its matching division problems:

$$3 \times 100 = 300 \qquad 300 \div 3 = 100 \qquad 300 \div 100 = 3$$

**RULE FOR DIVIDING BY 100:** A number is divisible by 100 if it ends with two zeros. To divide by 100, remove the two zeros.

**TAKE-HOME:** Practice Facts sheets, Travel Folders and flash cards.

**ASSIGNMENT:** Worksheets O, P and Q.

**QUOTIENT BINGO:** Give each student a 4" x 4" (10 x 10 cm) grid. Have each one write FREE in one space, wherever they choose. Using the numbers 0-10, have them write one number in each remaining square. They should use each number at least once, and no number should be used more than twice. Laminate the cards so that students can mark answers with an overhead marker or crayon. The teacher or a student calls out a division fact that has been studied. Students cover ONE answer on their board for that fact. First to get four in a row calls out "Quotient Bingo." Ask parents to donate gum or small education items as prizes.

**REMINDER:** The quotient is the answer in a division problem.

# QUOTIENT BINGO

# PRACTICE FACTS FOR 5s

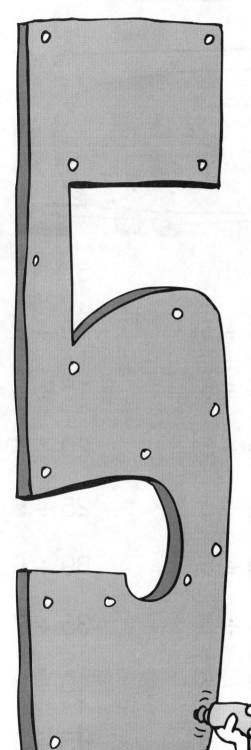

5 ÷ 5 = ___          5 ÷ 1 = ___

10 ÷ 5 = ___          10 ÷ 2 = ___

15 ÷ 5 = ___          15 ÷ 3 = ___

20 ÷ 5 = ___          20 ÷ 4 = ___

25 ÷ 5 = ___          25 ÷ 5 = ___

30 ÷ 5 = ___          30 ÷ 6 = ___

35 ÷ 5 = ___          35 ÷ 7 = ___

40 ÷ 5 = ___          40 ÷ 8 = ___

45 ÷ 5 = ___          45 ÷ 9 = ___

50 ÷ 5 = ___          50 ÷ 10 = ___

# TRAVEL FOLDER FOR 5s

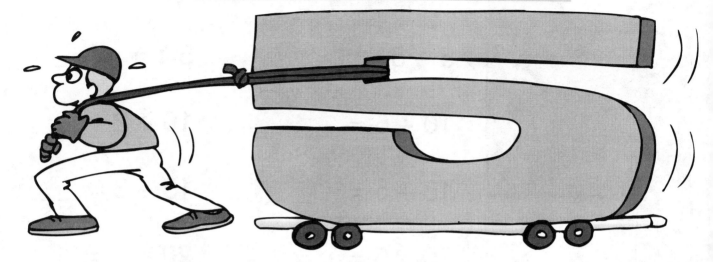

| | | | |
|---|---|---|---|
| 5 | 5 ÷ 5 = 1 | 5 ÷ 5 | 5 ÷ 1 |
| 10 | 10 ÷ 5 = 2 | 10 ÷ 5 | 10 ÷ 2 |
| 15 | 15 ÷ 5 = 3 | 15 ÷ 5 | 15 ÷ 3 |
| 20 | 20 ÷ 5 = 4 | 20 ÷ 5 | 20 ÷ 4 |
| 25 | 25 ÷ 5 = 5 | 25 ÷ 5 | 25 ÷ 5 |
| 30 | 30 ÷ 5 = 6 | 30 ÷ 5 | 30 ÷ 6 |
| 35 | 35 ÷ 5 = 7 | 35 ÷ 5 | 35 ÷ 7 |
| 40 | 40 ÷ 5 = 8 | 40 ÷ 5 | 40 ÷ 8 |
| 45 | 45 ÷ 5 = 9 | 45 ÷ 5 | 45 ÷ 9 |
| 50 | 50 ÷ 5 = 10 | 50 ÷ 5 | 50 ÷ 10 |

Name _____

# REVIEW

For each number given, make as many division problems as you can using that number as a dividend. The first one is done for you.

Remember these rules:

A number is divisible by nine if its numerals equal 9 when added together.

A number is divisible by two if it ends in 0, 2, 4, 6 or 8.

A number is divisible by 5 if it ends in 0 or 5.*

| $\overline{)9}$ | $\overline{)5}$ | $\overline{)18}$ | $\overline{)20}$ |
|---|---|---|---|
| $1\overline{)9}$ $\phantom{1}9$<br><br>$9\overline{)9}$ $\phantom{9}1$<br><br>$3\overline{)9}$ $\phantom{3}3$ | | | |

| $\overline{)32}$ | $\overline{)36}$ | $\overline{)40}$ | $\overline{)45}$ |
|---|---|---|---|
| | | | |

* Also, every number is divisible by itself and one!

# PRACTICE FACTS FOR 10s

10 ÷ 10 = ____

20 ÷ 10 = ____

30 ÷ 10 = ____

40 ÷ 10 = ____

50 ÷ 10 = ____

60 ÷ 10 = ____

70 ÷ 10 = ____

80 ÷ 10 = ____

90 ÷ 10 = ____

100 ÷ 10 = ____

10 ÷ 1 = ____

20 ÷ 2 = ____

30 ÷ 3 = ____

40 ÷ 4 = ____

50 ÷ 5 = ____

60 ÷ 6 = ____

70 ÷ 7 = ____

80 ÷ 8 = ____

90 ÷ 9 = ____

100 ÷ 10 = ____

# TRAVEL FOLDER FOR 10s

| | | | |
|---|---|---|---|
| 10 | 10 ÷ 10 = 1 | 10 ÷ 10 | 10 ÷ 1 |
| 20 | 20 ÷ 10 = 2 | 20 ÷ 10 | 20 ÷ 2 |
| 30 | 30 ÷ 10 = 3 | 30 ÷ 10 | 30 ÷ 3 |
| 40 | 40 ÷ 10 = 4 | 40 ÷ 10 | 40 ÷ 4 |
| 50 | 50 ÷ 10 = 5 | 50 ÷ 10 | 50 ÷ 5 |
| 60 | 60 ÷ 10 = 6 | 60 ÷ 10 | 60 ÷ 6 |
| 70 | 70 ÷ 10 = 7 | 70 ÷ 10 | 70 ÷ 7 |
| 80 | 80 ÷ 10 = 8 | 80 ÷ 10 | 80 ÷ 8 |
| 90 | 90 ÷ 10 = 9 | 90 ÷ 10 | 90 ÷ 9 |
| 100 | 100 ÷ 10 = 10 | 100 ÷ 10 | 100 ÷ 10 |

**73**

Name _____

# DIVIDING BY 5

1. 5)‾40‾  2. 1)‾5‾  3. 5)‾25‾  4. 3)‾15‾

5. 5)‾15‾  6. 9)‾45‾  7. 5)‾10‾  8. 10)‾50‾

9. 5)‾45‾  10. 4)‾20‾  11. 5)‾25‾  12. 7)‾35‾

13. 5)‾50‾  14. 5)‾5‾  15. 5)‾30‾  16. 6)‾30‾

17. 5)‾35‾  18. 8)‾40‾  19. 5)‾20‾  20. 2)‾10‾

# DIVIDING BY 10

21. 10)‾40‾  22. 1)‾10‾  23. 10)‾70‾  24. 10)‾20‾

25. 2)‾20‾  26. 5)‾50‾  27. 6)‾60‾  28. 10)‾10‾

29. 10)‾50‾  30. 3)‾30‾  31. 10)‾100‾  32. 10)‾30‾

33. 10)‾60‾  34. 4)‾40‾  35. 10)‾80‾  36. 7)‾70‾

37. 8)‾80‾  38. 10)‾90‾  39. 10)‾100‾  40. 9)‾90‾

**CHALLENGE:** Twenty people won money in the Sunnyside School drawing. Each one won $100.00. The school will pay the money in five equal parts. What is the total amount of money that will be paid in the first payment?

**74**

# DIVIDING BY 10s, 5s, 4s AND 8s

1. $5 \overline{)15}$     2. $10 \overline{)70}$     3. $4 \overline{)4}$     4. $5 \overline{)35}$

5. $5 \overline{)5}$     6. $8 \overline{)8}$     7. $4 \overline{)24}$     8. $4 \overline{)8}$

9. $10 \overline{)10}$     10. $8 \overline{)40}$     11. $8 \overline{)16}$     12. $4 \overline{)28}$

13. $5 \overline{)30}$     14. $5 \overline{)10}$     15. $8 \overline{)48}$     16. $10 \overline{)60}$

17. $5 \overline{)25}$     18. $8 \overline{)24}$     19. $10 \overline{)20}$     20. $5 \overline{)20}$

21. $4 \overline{)32}$     22. $8 \overline{)32}$     23. $10 \overline{)30}$     24. $4 \overline{)12}$

25. $5 \overline{)40}$     26. $8 \overline{)56}$     27. $10 \overline{)50}$     28. $4 \overline{)16}$

29. $10 \overline{)40}$     30. $5 \overline{)45}$     31. $8 \overline{)64}$     32. $4 \overline{)36}$

33. $10 \overline{)80}$     34. $5 \overline{)50}$     35. $10 \overline{)100}$     36. $4 \overline{)40}$

37. $10 \overline{)90}$     38. $8 \overline{)80}$     39. $8 \overline{)72}$     40. $4 \overline{)20}$

| 6 |   | 8 |
|---|---|---|
|   | 5 |   |
| 2 |   |   |

**CHALLENGE**: Here is a magic square. In every row of three numbers, down, across or diagonal, the sum is the same. Fill in the numbers.

# LESSON PLAN 8

**OBJECTIVE:** Dividing by 3 and 6. Students will learn division facts for three and six. They will also learn facts in which the answer is three and facts in which the answer is six.

**INTRODUCTION:** Have the class chant the 5s division facts and the 10s division facts. (Optional: Teacher gives the division fact and the class calls out the answer.)

Review some of the other groups as needed.

**REVIEW:** Ask students for the multiplication facts for three. Write them on the board.

3 x 1 = 3    3 x 2 = 6    3 x 3 = 9 and so on.

**DIVIDING BY 3:** Have the class give the matching division facts for each 3s multiplication facts:

| | | |
|---|---|---|
| 3 x 1 = 3 | 3 ÷ 3 = 1 | 3 ÷ 1 = 3 |
| 3 x 2 = 6 | 6 ÷ 3 = 2 | 6 ÷ 2 = 3 |
| 3 x 3 = 9 | 9 ÷ 3 = 3 | 9 ÷ 3 = 3 |
| 3 x 4 = 12 | 12 ÷ 3 = 4 | 12 ÷ 4 = 3 and so on. |

Cross off all facts which have already been learned so students will see that they only have a few to learn.

**DIVIDING BY 6:** Go through the same process for the 6s.

**NOTE:** If students are having problems with these groups, take a little time out and have them practice counting by threes and by sixes. Counting by sixes uses every other number in the counting by threes sequence. Also, when you count by six, you use every even number that is divisible by three.

**HOMEWORK:** Use Practice Facts sheets, Travel Folders, flash cards, quotient beads and worksheets as described in previous lessons.

**MATERIALS:** Flash Cards (pages 25-34), Practice Facts for 3s (page 77), Travel Folder for 3s (page78), Practice Facts for 6s (page 79), Travel Folder for 6s (page 80), Worksheets R and S (pages 81 and 82)

**WORKSHEET R:** The goal of question 5 is to help students see the pattern in numbers divisible by 3 and divisible by 6. Have students look at the numbers divisible by three: 3, 6, 9, 12, 15, 18, 21, 24, 27, 30. Starting with 12, look at the sums of the numerals:

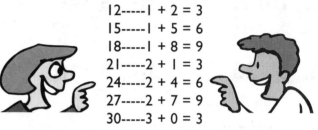

```
12-----1 + 2 = 3
15-----1 + 5 = 6
18-----1 + 8 = 9
21-----2 + 1 = 3
24-----2 + 4 = 6
27-----2 + 7 = 9
30-----3 + 0 = 3
```

This is a good way to tell if a number is divisible by three:

**RULE:** A number is divisible by three if the numerals will add up to 3, 6 or 9.

Here are the numbers divisible by 6 from 1-30: 6, 12, 18, 24, 30. These numbers are all divisible by 3 and they are also even numbers.

**RULE:** A number is divisible by 6 if it is an even number and its numerals add up to 3, 6 or 9.

## PLAYING CARD DIVISION DRILL:

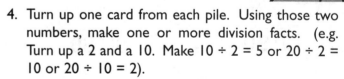

1. One- or two-player games.

2. Remove face cards.

3. Divide cards into two equal piles.

4. Turn up one card from each pile. Using those two numbers, make one or more division facts. (e.g. Turn up a 2 and a 10. Make 10 ÷ 2 = 5 or 20 ÷ 2 = 10 or 20 ÷ 10 = 2).

5. For a two-player game, players can take turns or they can play it like Slapjack with the first player to call out a fact getting the two cards. Also, set a time limit and stop at the end of the time and count cards to determine the winner.

6. Use page 9 to help you think of division facts if necessary.

# PRACTICE FACTS FOR 3s

| | |
|---|---|
| 3 ÷ 3 = ___ | 3 ÷ 1 = ___ |
| 6 ÷ 3 = ___ | 6 ÷ 2 = ___ |
| 9 ÷ 3 = ___ | 9 ÷ 3 = ___ |
| 12 ÷ 3 = ___ | 12 ÷ 4 = ___ |
| 15 ÷ 3 = ___ | 15 ÷ 5 = ___ |
| 18 ÷ 3 = ___ | 18 ÷ 6 = ___ |
| 21 ÷ 3 = ___ | 21 ÷ 7 = ___ |
| 24 ÷ 3 = ___ | 24 ÷ 8 = ___ |
| 27 ÷ 3 = ___ | 27 ÷ 9 = ___ |
| 30 ÷ 3 = ___ | 30 ÷ 10 = ___ |

# TRAVEL FOLDER FOR 3s

| | | | |
|---|---|---|---|
| 3 | 3 ÷ 3 = 1 | 3 ÷ 3 | 3 ÷ 1 |
| 6 | 6 ÷ 3 = 2 | 6 ÷ 3 | 6 ÷ 2 |
| 9 | 9 ÷ 3 = 3 | 9 ÷ 3 | 9 ÷ 3 |
| 12 | 12 ÷ 3 = 4 | 12 ÷ 3 | 12 ÷ 4 |
| 15 | 15 ÷ 3 = 5 | 15 ÷ 3 | 15 ÷ 5 |
| 18 | 18 ÷ 3 = 6 | 18 ÷ 3 | 18 ÷ 6 |
| 21 | 21 ÷ 3 = 7 | 21 ÷ 3 | 21 ÷ 7 |
| 24 | 24 ÷ 3 = 8 | 24 ÷ 3 | 24 ÷ 8 |
| 27 | 27 ÷ 3 = 9 | 27 ÷ 3 | 27 ÷ 9 |
| 30 | 30 ÷ 3 = 10 | 30 ÷ 3 | 30 ÷ 10 |

Name _____

# PRACTICE FACTS FOR 6s

$6 \div 6 =$ ___

$12 \div 6 =$ ___

$18 \div 6 =$ ___

$24 \div 6 =$ ___

$30 \div 6 =$ ___

$36 \div 6 =$ ___

$42 \div 6 =$ ___

$48 \div 6 =$ ___

$54 \div 6 =$ ___

$60 \div 6 =$ ___

$6 \div 1 =$ ___

$12 \div 2 =$ ___

$18 \div 3 =$ ___

$24 \div 4 =$ ___

$30 \div 5 =$ ___

$36 \div 6 =$ ___

$42 \div 7 =$ ___

$48 \div 8 =$ ___

$54 \div 9 =$ ___

$60 \div 10 =$ ___

Name _____

# TRAVEL FOLDER FOR 6s

| 6 | $6 \div 6 =$ ___ | $6 \div 6$ | $6 \div 1$ |
| 12 | $12 \div 6 =$ ___ | $12 \div 6$ | $12 \div 2$ |
| 18 | $18 \div 6 =$ ___ | $18 \div 6$ | $18 \div 3$ |
| 24 | $24 \div 6 =$ ___ | $24 \div 6$ | $24 \div 4$ |
| 30 | $30 \div 6 =$ ___ | $30 \div 6$ | $30 \div 5$ |
| 36 | $36 \div 6 =$ ___ | $36 \div 6$ | $36 \div 6$ |
| 42 | $42 \div 6 =$ ___ | $42 \div 6$ | $24 \div 7$ |
| 48 | $48 \div 6 =$ ___ | $48 \div 6$ | $48 \div 8$ |
| 54 | $54 \div 6 =$ ___ | $54 \div 6$ | $54 \div 9$ |
| 60 | $60 \div 6 =$ ___ | $60 \div 6$ | $60 \div 10$ |

# WEB WORK

In each web, the center number is the dividend. The six numbers around it are the divisors. Write the answers in the outer sections of the webs. Two have been done for you.

1.
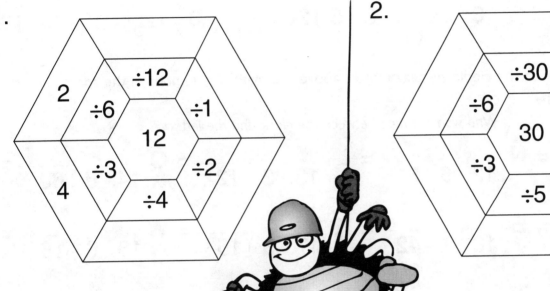

2.

3.
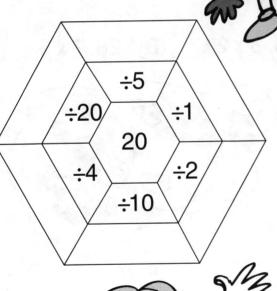

4.
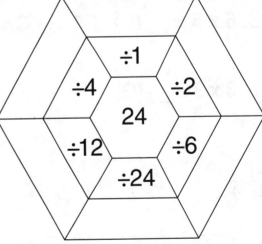

5. On the back of this page write the numbers 1-30. Circle every number divisible by 3. Put an X above every number divisible by 6. Do you see any patterns in these numbers? Make up a rule for numbers divisible by 3 and numbers divisible by 6.

# DIVIDING BY 3s AND 6s

1. $6\overline{)48}$   2. $3\overline{)30}$   3. $3\overline{)9}$   4. $6\overline{)36}$   5. $8\overline{)48}$

6. $3\overline{)21}$   7. $6\overline{)54}$   8. $6\overline{)30}$   9. $6\overline{)12}$   10. $3\overline{)18}$

To find the answer to this riddle, put each letter above the matching number in the spaces at the bottom of the page.

*Who won the race between the clock and the lettuce?*

11. $3\overline{)6}^{2}$ = N   12. $6\overline{)6}$ = L   13. $3\overline{)12}$ = O   14. $6\overline{)60}$ = U

15. $6\overline{)42}$ = E   16. $7\overline{)42}$ = K   17. $3\overline{)15}$ = W   18. $6\overline{)18}$ = S

19. $3\overline{)24}$ = T   20. $3\overline{)27}$ = H   21. $6 \times 3 =$ ___ (A)   22. $6 \times 2 =$ ___ (I)

23. $6 \times 5 =$ ___ (C)   24. $5 \times 3 =$ ___ (D)   25. $8 \times 2 =$ ___ (B)   26. $7 \times 3 =$ ___ (R)

27. $8 \times 3 =$ ___ (G)

$\dfrac{N}{2}\ \overline{4}$   $\overline{4}\ \dfrac{N}{2}\ \overline{7}$   $\overline{6}\ \dfrac{N}{2}\ \overline{4}\ \overline{5}\ \overline{3}$ .

$\overline{8}\ \overline{9}\ \overline{7}$   $\overline{1}\ \overline{7}\ \overline{8}\ \overline{8}\ \overline{10}\ \overline{30}\ \overline{7}$   $\overline{12}\ \overline{3}$   $\overline{18}$   $\overline{9}\ \overline{7}\ \overline{18}\ \overline{15}$ ,

$\overline{16}\ \overline{10}\ \overline{8}$   $\overline{8}\ \overline{9}\ \overline{7}$   $\overline{30}\ \overline{1}\ \overline{4}\ \overline{30}\ \overline{6}$   $\overline{12}\ \overline{3}$   $\overline{3}\ \overline{8}\ \overline{12}\ \overline{1}\ \overline{1}$

$\overline{21}\ \overline{10}\ \dfrac{N}{2}\ \dfrac{N}{2}\ \overline{12}\ \dfrac{N}{2}\ \overline{24}$ .

# LESSON PLAN 9

**OBJECTIVE:** Dividing by 7. Students will learn the division facts for seven. They will also learn facts in which the answer is seven.

**MATERIALS:** Flash Cards (pages 25-34), Practice Facts for 7s (page 84), Travel Folder for 7s (page 85), Worksheet T (page 86)

**INTRODUCTION:** Have the entire class chant the threes and sixes division facts. (Optional: Teacher says the division fact and the class calls out the answer.) Review any of the other groups that the class needs to review.

**REVIEW:** Since sevens are so tricky for students to recall, I recommend using a wall chart or overhead transparency of the Base 10 Counting Chart at this time. Count by sevens and circle every seventh number to review the multiples of seven. Using those numbers, ask students to give all the multiplication facts for seven. Write them in order on the board.

$7 \times 1 = 7$

$7 \times 2 = 14$

$7 \times 3 = 21$

$7 \times 4 = 28$ and so on

**DIVIDING BY 7:** Have the class give the matching division facts for each multiplication fact:

$7 \times 1 = 7$    $7 \div 7 = 1$    $7 \div 1 = 7$

$7 \times 2 = 14$   $14 \div 7 = 2$   $14 \div 2 = 7$

$7 \times 3 = 21$   $21 \div 7 = 3$   $21 \div 3 = 7$ and so on.

Have the class name all facts which they have already learned and cross them off. You should be able to cross off all the facts. All these facts have been learned in previous lessons. The sevens are frequently the most difficult for students to remember. For this reason, we will study them as a group even though they are all review.

**CALENDARS:** Point out to students that the three numbers under the seven on any calendar are all divisible by seven. They are 14, 21 and 28. Whenever the students see a calendar, they can be reminded of the first four numbers that are divisible by seven.

**TAKE-HOME:** Use Practice Facts sheets, Travel Folders, flash cards, quotient beads and worksheets as described in previous lessons.

# PRACTICE FACTS FOR 7s

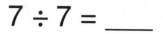

$7 \div 7 =$ ___          $7 \div 1 =$ ___

$14 \div 7 =$ ___          $14 \div 2 =$ ___

$21 \div 7 =$ ___          $21 \div 3 =$ ___

$28 \div 7 =$ ___          $28 \div 4 =$ ___

$35 \div 7 =$ ___          $35 \div 5 =$ ___

$42 \div 7 =$ ___          $42 \div 6 =$ ___

$49 \div 7 =$ ___          $49 \div 7 =$ ___

$56 \div 7 =$ ___          $56 \div 8 =$ ___

$63 \div 7 =$ ___          $63 \div 9 =$ ___

$70 \div 7 =$ ___          $70 \div 10 =$ ___

Name _____

# TRAVEL FOLDER FOR 7s

| 7 | $7 \div 7 = 1$ | $7 \div 7$ | $7 \div 1$ |
| 14 | $14 \div 7 = 2$ | $14 \div 7$ | $14 \div 2$ |
| 21 | $21 \div 7 = 3$ | $21 \div 7$ | $21 \div 3$ |
| 28 | $28 \div 7 = 4$ | $28 \div 7$ | $28 \div 4$ |
| 35 | $35 \div 7 = 5$ | $35 \div 7$ | $35 \div 5$ |
| 42 | $42 \div 7 = 6$ | $42 \div 7$ | $42 \div 6$ |
| 49 | $49 \div 7 = 7$ | $49 \div 7$ | $49 \div 7$ |
| 56 | $56 \div 7 = 8$ | $56 \div 7$ | $56 \div 8$ |
| 63 | $63 \div 7 = 9$ | $63 \div 7$ | $63 \div 9$ |
| 70 | $70 \div 7 = 10$ | $70 \div 7$ | $70 \div 10$ |

Name _____

# DIVIDING BY 7

1. 2)‾1‾4‾    2. 7)‾6‾3‾    3. 3)‾2‾1‾    4. 7)‾1‾4‾    5. 7)‾7‾0‾

6. 4)‾2‾8‾    7. 5)‾3‾5‾    8. 7)‾7‾    9. 8)‾5‾6‾    10. 7)‾4‾9‾

11. 7)‾2‾1‾    12. 6)‾4‾2‾    13. 7)‾3‾5‾    14. 1)‾7‾    15. 7)‾5‾6‾

16. 7)‾4‾9‾    17. 7)‾2‾8‾    18. 9)‾6‾3‾    19. 7)‾4‾2‾    20. 10)‾7‾0‾

21. Baseball season lasts 63 days. What is the total number of weeks in the season?

22. Seven students volunteered to help a needy family. They must raise $56.00 for a Christmas dinner. If each student raises the same amount, how much money must each student raise?

23. Mrs. Jabar's class is cutting out felt letters for a banner. The felt is 49" long. If the felt is cut into 7 equal pieces, how long is each piece?

**CHALLENGE:** What is the length of the original piece of felt in feet and inches?

Review using T-table quizzes. Have students work in pairs with flash cards. Play Quotient Bingo as a class or in pairs. Have students work with RACKO™ cards, quotient beads or a Trivial Pursuit™ game to avoid monotony.

## RACKO™ CHALLENGE:

Now that students have learned all the division facts, use all the RACKO™ cards. Turn over a card. Students should give at least one division fact using that number as the dividend. If that number can only be divided by itself and one, it is a prime. See Primes Activity Sheet on page 88.

When you feel that sufficient time has been allowed for review, give the Division Assessment (pages 90-92) to the class.

After grading, give each student a copy of page 9. Have students highlight all facts they got correct on the assessment. They should continue studying the ones they missed and retake the assessment until they reach mastery.

*Math Phonics™–Division* materials can be used for drill and review for the next year or so. Students will probably need some review for a while.

## NOTE TO TEACHERS

### PRIMES ACTIVITY SHEET:

The next two pages—Primes Activity Sheet and Primes Games—can be copied and used as a worksheet with each student finding primes alone. Another approach would be to do the primes activity in class as a group with the teacher leading the discussion.

This is optional for beginning students of division. This is an activity that is more often used in seventh grade or above. However, younger students can understand and learn primes very well. Knowing primes will help them in ways that are mentioned on the following page.

# PRIMES ACTIVITY SHEET

An understanding of primes and a basic knowledge of primes is extremely useful in solving many types of math problems. In adding fractions, primes help in finding least common multiples–common denominators. In multiplication of fractions, knowledge of primes helps keep the numbers small and helps in reducing fractions to lowest terms. In algebra, primes are helpful in solving complex equations.

**Primes:** A prime is a number which is divisible by exactly two numbers–itself and one. One is not considered a prime.

**Composite:** Any number which is divisible by three or more numbers is called a composite. Four is a composite because it is divisible by 1, 2 and 4. 1, 2 and 4 are called factors of the number 4.

**PRIMES ACTIVITY:** Using the Base 10 Counting Chart, find the primes between 1 and 150 by following these steps:

1. Circle 2 because it is a prime. Cross out all multiples of 2–all the even numbers. Use a red pen or marker.

2. Circle 3 because it is a prime. Cross out all the multiples of 3–that is 3, 6, 9 and so on. Use blue pen, marker or crayon.

3. 4 has already been crossed out so we know it is not a prime.

4. 5 has not yet been crossed off so we know it is a prime. Circle 5. Cross off all multiples of 5. Use green pen, marker or crayon.

5. 6 has been crossed out because 6 is divisible by 2. Do we need to check the multiples of 6? No. All of them have been crossed off in red and in blue because 6 is divisible by 2 and 3.

6. 7 has not been crossed off. This means 7 has no factor smaller than itself except 1. 7 is a prime. Circle 7 and check the multiples of 7. Cross them off with yellow. Has 7 x 2 been crossed off yet? Yes, in red because it is divisible by 2. What about 7 x 3? 7 x 4? All have been crossed off up to 7 x 7. Cross that one off. What about 7 x 8? It has been crossed off in red because it is divisible by 2. What about 7 x 9? It has been crossed off in blue because 9 is divisible by 3 and 7 x 9 is divisible by 3.

7. Do we need to check numbers divisible by 8? No, all of them have been crossed off in red because they are divisible by 2. Do we need to check numbers divisible by 9? No, all of them have been crossed off in blue because they are divisible by 3.

8. Continue this process until you reach 149–the last prime before 150. Write all the primes you found. There are 35 primes less than 150.

# PRIMES GAMES

**PLAYING CARD PRIMES:** This is played like Slapjack. Two-player game. Remove face cards. Deal out all the cards into two piles.

Since the numbered cards only go up to 10, the only primes used will be 2, 3, 5 and 7.

Players take turns turning over one card at a time. Whenever a prime is turned over, the first player to slap the prime gets that card and all the cards in the pile under it.

Play until one player runs out of cards, or until time runs out. Set a time limit before beginning if you wish.

**RACKO™ PRIMES:** Use a RACKO™ deck. Play the game like Slapjack. Since numbers go up to 60, there will be more primes to slap. Here are the primes up to 60: 2, 3, 5, 7, 11, 13, 17, 19, 23, 29, 31, 37, 41, 43, 47, 53, 59.

The game could also be played with all the cards up to 20. There would be eight primes in that group. The primes less than 20 will be most frequently used.

# DIVISION ASSESSMENT

1.  **50 ÷ 5 =** ____

2.  **2 ÷ 2 =** ____

3.  **16 ÷ 8 =** ____

4.  **4 ÷ 4 =** ____

5.  **18 ÷ 9 =** ____

6.  **5)25**

7.  **4)12**

8.  **9 ÷ 9 =** ____

9.  **1 ÷ 1 =** ____

10. **4 ÷ 2 =** ____

11. **5)20**

12. **9)27**

13. **2)6**

14. **4)36**

15. **4)0**

16. **4)16**

17. **8)48**

18. **8)8**

19. **9)36**

20. **4)8**

21. **5)15**

22. **8)24**

23. **9)45**

24. **5)0**

25. **8)32**

26. **5)45**

27. **9)54**

28. **2)8**

29. **9)63**

30. **2)10**

31. **9)72**

32. **4)28**

33. **4)20**

34. **9)81**

35. **2)16**

36. **2)12**

37. **9)0**

38. **4)32**

39. **2)14**

# DIVISION ASSESSMENT

40. $2\overline{)18}$

41. $8\overline{)56}$

42. $5\overline{)40}$

43. $4\overline{)24}$

44. $8\overline{)0}$

45. $2\overline{)0}$

46. $5\overline{)30}$

47. $5\overline{)35}$

48. $8\overline{)64}$

49. $8\overline{)80}$

50. $8\overline{)72}$

51. $3\overline{)6}$

52. $1\overline{)0}$

53. $3\overline{)12}$

54. $10\overline{)70}$

55. $3\overline{)3}$

56. $6\overline{)6}$

57. $1\overline{)9}$

58. $3\overline{)9}$

59. $5\overline{)5}$

60. $10\overline{)20}$

61. $7\overline{)56}$

62. $3\overline{)15}$

63. $1\overline{)2}$

64. $10\overline{)10}$

65. $7\overline{)7}$

66. $10\overline{)0}$

67. $3\overline{)18}$

68. $10\overline{)80}$

69. $1\overline{)3}$

70. $10\overline{)30}$

71. $7\overline{)49}$

72. $1\overline{)8}$

73. $7\overline{)63}$

74. $3\overline{)21}$

75. $3\overline{)27}$

76. $7\overline{)42}$

77. $10\overline{)40}$

78. $7\overline{)0}$

**91**

Name _____

# DIVISION ASSESSMENT

79. $1 \overline{)4}$

80. $3 \overline{)24}$

81. $7 \overline{)35}$

82. $10 \overline{)90}$

83. $1 \overline{)6}$

84. $10 \overline{)60}$

85. $1 \overline{)5}$

86. $10 \overline{)100}$

87. $1 \overline{)7}$

88. $6 \overline{)0}$

89. $6 \overline{)36}$

90. $3 \overline{)0}$

91. $7 \overline{)28}$

92. $6 \overline{)54}$

93. $6 \overline{)42}$

94. $6 \overline{)12}$

95. $6 \overline{)24}$

96. $7 \overline{)21}$

97. $6 \overline{)48}$

98. $6 \overline{)18}$

99. $7 \overline{)14}$

100. $6 \overline{)60}$

101. $4 \overline{)40}$

102. $5 \overline{)10}$

103. $9 \overline{)90}$

104. $8 \overline{)40}$

105. $2 \overline{)20}$

106. $3 \overline{)30}$

107. $1 \overline{)10}$

108. $6 \overline{)30}$

109. $7 \overline{)70}$

110. $10 \overline{)50}$

# RULES AND GAMES

**DIVIDING BY 1:** When a number is divided by one, the number stays the same. (e.g. 8 ÷ 1 = 8)

**DIVIDING BY 2:** A number is evenly divisible by two if it ends in 0, 2, 4, 6 or 8. The doubles in addition can be used to learn to divide by two. (8 + 8 = 16   16 ÷ 2 = 8)

**DIVIDING BY 3:** A number is divisible by three if the sum of its numerals is 3, 6 or 9.

**DIVIDING BY 4:** Students should learn the pattern in numbers divisible by four:

|    |    |    |    |    |
|----|----|----|----|----|
| 4, | 8, | 12, | 16, | 20, |
| 24, | 28, | 32, | 36, | 40 |

**DIVIDING BY 5:** Numbers divisible by five must must end in 0 or 5. If the dividend ends in 5, the answer will be an odd number. If the dividend ends in 0, the answer will be an even number.

**DIVIDING BY 6:** A number is divisible by six if it is an even number and the sum of its numerals is 3, 6 or 9.

**DIVIDING BY 7:** Numbers divisible by seven must be learned by familiarity. There is not a convenient pattern. Remember the mnemonic device 5, 6, 7, 8 for 56 ÷ 7 = 8. Remember that the numbers under the 7 on a calendar are divisible by seven. They are 14, 21 and 28.

**DIVIDING BY 8:** Numbers divisible by eight must be even numbers. Numbers divisible by eight have a pattern in the 1s place—

|    |    |    |    |    |
|----|----|----|----|----|
| 8, | 16, | 24, | 32, | 40, |
| 48, | 56, | 64, | 72, | 80 |

**DIVIDING BY 9:** A number is divisible by nine if the sum of its numerals is nine. Numbers divisible by nine can be put into pairs—18 and 81, 27 and 72, 36 and 63, 45 and 54. When dividing a two-digit number by nine, look at the numeral in the 10s place—add one—that is the answer.

**DIVIDING BY 10:** A number is divisible by 10 if it ends in a zero. To divide by 10, remove the zero.

**ZERO:** Zero divided by any number always equals zero. This makes sense. If I have zero dollars and share with a friend, we both have zero—0 ÷ 2 = 0. If I share with nine friends, we all have zero—0 ÷ 9 = 0.

Dividing by zero is not allowed—it is not defined. In this problem $0\overline{)10}$ , there is no number times zero that equal 10.

# GAMES AND ACTIVITIES

**TRIVIAL PURSUIT™:** Use division flash cards in place of questions.

**QUOTIENT BEADS:** Used to demonstrate division facts. See Lesson Plan 4 (page 40).

**RACKO™:** To study one group of facts, take out all number cards divisible by number. See Lesson Plan 5 (page 49) for instructions.

**RACKO™ CHALLENGE:** See Lesson Plan 10 (page 87) for instructions.

**QUOTIENT BINGO:** See Lesson Plan 7 (page 67) for instructions.

**PLAYING CARD DIVISION DRILL:** See Lesson Plan 8 (page 76) for instructions.

**PLAYING CARD PRIMES AND RACKO™ PRIMES:** See Lesson Plan 10 for instructions (page 89).

## DEAR PARENTS,

# CONGRATULATIONS!

Your child mastered all the division facts! This is a very important math skill, and I am happy that our class is doing so well at this time.

Please remember to review or drill every week or two. Going through the flash cards is an excellent way to review. Make two piles—one pile of the facts your child can say correctly and another of the ones he or she has missed. Continue to work on the "misses." If your child misses several in one group, get out that Travel Folder and review. Good luck!

Sincerely,

# DEAR PARENTS,

We will start a review unit on division tomorrow. Please practice the math facts tonight so the review will go well. Remember to use the Travel Folders, Practice Facts sheets, flash cards and games.

Sincerely,

**94**

# BASE 10 COUNTING CHART

| 1 | 2 | 3 | 4 | 5 | 6 | 7 | 8 | 9 | 10 |
|---|---|---|---|---|---|---|---|---|----|
| 11 | 12 | 13 | 14 | 15 | 16 | 17 | 18 | 19 | 20 |
| 21 | 22 | 23 | 24 | 25 | 26 | 27 | 28 | 29 | 30 |
| 31 | 32 | 33 | 34 | 35 | 36 | 37 | 38 | 39 | 40 |
| 41 | 42 | 43 | 44 | 45 | 46 | 47 | 48 | 49 | 50 |
| 51 | 52 | 53 | 54 | 55 | 56 | 57 | 58 | 59 | 60 |
| 61 | 62 | 63 | 64 | 65 | 66 | 67 | 68 | 69 | 70 |
| 71 | 72 | 73 | 74 | 75 | 76 | 77 | 78 | 79 | 80 |
| 81 | 82 | 83 | 84 | 85 | 86 | 87 | 88 | 89 | 90 |
| 91 | 92 | 93 | 94 | 95 | 96 | 97 | 98 | 99 | 100 |
| 101 | 102 | 103 | 104 | 105 | 106 | 107 | 108 | 109 | 110 |
| 111 | 112 | 113 | 114 | 115 | 116 | 117 | 118 | 119 | 120 |
| 121 | 122 | 123 | 124 | 125 | 126 | 127 | 128 | 129 | 130 |
| 131 | 132 | 133 | 134 | 135 | 136 | 137 | 138 | 139 | 140 |
| 141 | 142 | 143 | 144 | 145 | 146 | 147 | 148 | 149 | 150 |

# ANSWER KEY

## Worksheet A, page 12

Challenge: a. 20, b. 20, c. 30, d. 40, e. 30

## Worksheet B, page 13

Challenge: a. 90, b. 90, c. 70

## Worksheet C, page 20

Challenge: Day 5 = 32 cookies; all seven days = 128 cookies

## Worksheet D, page 21

Challenge: a. 40, b. 400, c. 300
Extra Challenge: inverse functions

## Worksheet E, page 37

Challenge: a. 40, b. 400, c. 30, d. 33, e. 300, f. 50, g. 51, h. 500, i. 80, j. 90
Extra Challenge: dividend, divisor, quotient

## Worksheet F, page 38

Challenge: $11^2 = 121$, $12^2 = 144$, $13^2 = 169$, $14^2 = 196$, $15^2 = 225$

## Worksheet G, page 43

Challenge: She needs 36 feet. Each wall is 9 feet or 3 yards.

## Worksheet H, page 44

Challenge: a. 12 rows; b. 9, 18, 27, 36, 45, 54, 63, 72, 81, 90, 99, 108, 117, 126, 135, 144, 153, 162, 171, 180, 189, 198

## Worksheet I, page 52

Challenge: 15, 18, the box process takes a number times 3

## Mid-Unit Assessment for Squares, 9s and 2s; page 55

Challenge: a. 60; b. 90; c. 600; d. 36 pizzas, 6 pizzas

## Worksheet K, page 60

Challenge: $1,000

## Worksheet L, page 61

Challenge: 48

## Worksheet M, page 64

Challenge: a. 8, 16, 24, 32, 40, 48, 56, 64, 72, 80, 88, 96, 104, 112, 120, 128, 136, 144; b. 36, 72, 108, 144; c. 72, 144

## Worksheet N, page 65

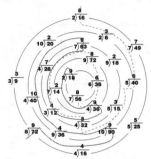

## Worksheet O, page 71

| )9 | )5 | )18 | )20 |
|---|---|---|---|
| 9 1)9 1 9)9 3 3)9 | 1 5)5 5 1)5 | 18 1 1)18 18)18 9 2)18 6 3)18 | 20 1 1)20 20)20 5 4)20 10 2)20 |
| | | 1 18)18 2 9)18 3 6)18 | 1 20)20 4 5)20 2 10)20 |

| )32 | )36 | )40 | )45 |
|---|---|---|---|
| 32 1)32 1 32)32 16 2)32 8 4)32 | 36 1)36 1 36)36 18 2)36 12 3)36 | 9 4)36 40 1)40 1 40)40 20 2)40 6 6)36 10 4)40 | 8 5)40 45 1)45 1 45)45 5 8)40 9 5)45 |
| | 2 18)36 3 12)36 | 2 20)40 10)40 4 | 3 15)45 5 9)45 |

## Worksheet P, page 74

Challenge: $400

## Worksheet Q, page 75

Challenge:

| 6 | 1 | 8 |
|---|---|---|
| 7 | 5 | 3 |
| 2 | 9 | 4 |

## Worksheet S, page 82

Answer: No one knows. The lettuce is ahead, but the clock is still running.

## Worksheet T, page 86

Challenge: 4 feet, 1 inch

## Primes Activity Sheet, page 88

2, 3, 5, 7, 11, 13, 17, 19, 23, 29, 31, 37, 41, 43, 47, 53, 59, 61, 67, 71, 73, 79, 83, 89, 97, 101, 103, 107, 109, 113, 127, 131, 137, 139, 149